THE QUOTABLE SOUL

Inspiring Quotations
Crossing Time and Culture

CLAUDIA SETZER, Ph.D.

A Stonesong Press Book

John Wiley & Sons, Inc.
New York · Chichester · Brisbane · Toronto · Singapore

Copyright © 1994 by The Stonesong Press, Inc.
Published by John Wiley & Sons, Inc.

Library of Congress Cataloging-in-Publication Data

The quotable soul : inspiring quotations crossing time
    and culture / [compiled by] Claudia Setzer.
        p.   cm.
    "A Stonesong Press book."
    Includes bibliographical references (p.   ) and index.
    ISBN 0-471-30829-3 (alk. paper)
    1. Spiritual life—Quotations, maxims, etc.   2. Religion—
Quotations, maxims, etc.   I. Setzer, Claudia
BL624.S67286   1994
200—dc20   93-36589

Printed in the United States of America

10 9 8 7 6 5 4 3 2 1

Preface

We are passing through a time in our history when religion is a crucial element in global affairs. In choosing quotes, I have tried to honor both the diversity of world religions as well as the varying points of view within those religions. Readers will find in these quotes joy and pain, anger and hope. They will also see that the spirit speaks in many languages.

My sincere thanks go to my editor, Sheree Bykofsky, who gently but tenaciously saw this book through and to Paul Fargis who conceived of this project and graciously supported it. Thanks also go to my children, Leora and Alexander, who provided constant joy and balance and never disturbed the many piles of paper.

—Claudia Setzer

Contents

CONTENTS

Action

*T*hrough faith man experiences the meaning of the world;
through action he is to give to it meaning.

LEO BAECK

*T*o act is to be committed, and to be committed is to be in
danger.

JAMES BALDWIN

*L*et not the fruit of action be your motive to action. Your
business is with action alone, not with the fruit of action.

BHAGAVAD-GITA

*O*nly by his actions can a man make himself/his life whole.
. . . You are responsible for what you have done and people
whom you have influenced.

MARGARET BOURKE-WHITE

*W*hen a man surrenders himself as a slave to the Divine Lord
he realizes at the end that all his actions are the actions of God.
He loses his mind-ness. This is what is meant by "doing the
will of God."

PAUL BRUNTON

*M*an's action is enclosed in God's action, but it is still real action.

MARTIN BUBER

*T*he great man is sparing in words but prodigal in deeds.

CONFUCIUS

*S*ervice is the rent each of us pays for living—the very purpose of life and not something you do in your spare time or after you have reached your personal goals.

MARIAN WRIGHT EDELMAN

*I*n our era, the road to holiness necessarily passes through the world of action.

DAG HAMMARSKJÖLD

*A*n action, to have moral worth, must be done from duty.

IMMANUEL KANT

*S*ick or well, blind or seeing, bond or free, we are here for a purpose and however we are situated, we please God better with useful deeds than with many prayers or pious resignation.

HELEN KELLER

*M*en must be decided on what they will not do, and then they are able to act with vigor in what they ought to do.

MENCIUS

*T*he most excellent of all actions is to befriend any one on God's account, and to be at enmity with whosoever is the enemy of God.

QUR'ĀN

The more merciful Acts thou dost, the more Mercy thou wilt receive.

WILLIAM PENN

The question is: Who will get to heaven first—the man who talks or the man who acts?

MELVIN B. TOLSON

"Let God do it all," someone will say; but if man folds his arms, God will go to sleep.

MIGUEL DE UNAMUNO Y JUGO

Afterlife/Heaven & Hell

*H*ell has three doors: lust, rage, and greed.

BHAGAVAD-GITA

*I*t is only when one loves life and the earth so much that one may believe in the resurrection and a new world.

DIETRICH BONHOEFFER

*W*hen you make the two one, and when you make the inside like the outside and the outside like the inside, and the above like the below, and when you make the male and the female one and the same . . . then you will enter [the Kingdom].

GNOSTIC GOSPEL OF THOMAS

*H*eaven: The Coney Island of the Christian imagination.

ELBERT HUBBARD

*H*ell is paved with good intentions.

SAMUEL JOHNSON

*A*ll that is sweet, delightful, and amiable in this world . . . is nothing else but Heaven breaking through the veil of this world.

WILLIAM LAW

*B*lessed are the poor in spirit, for theirs is the kingdom
of heaven.

MATTHEW 5:3

*H*ow anyone can believe in eternal punishment . . . or in any
soul which God has made being "lost," and also believe in the
love, nay, even in the justice of God, is a mystery indeed.

C. G. MONTEFIORE

*A*nd I have warned you of a fire that flames! None shall broil
thereon, but the most wretched, who says it is a lie and turns
his back. But the pious shall be kept away from it.

QUR'ĀN

*F*or observe, that to hope for Paradise is to live in Paradise, a
very different thing from actually getting there.

VITA SACKVILLE-WEST

Anger

*I*f you have respect for your enemy instead of anger, your compassion will develop.

FOURTEENTH DALAI LAMA

*H*e who holds back rising anger like a rolling chariot, him I call a real driver; other people are but holding the reins.

DHAMMAPADA

I have learnt through bitter experience the one supreme lesson to conserve my anger, and as heat conserved is transmuted into energy, even so our anger controlled can be transmuted into a power which can move the world.

MOHANDAS K. GANDHI

*T*he God I believe in is not so fragile that you hurt Him by being angry at Him, or so petty that He will hold it against you for being upset with Him.

HAROLD KUSHNER

*W*hen anger spreads through the breast, guard thy tongue from barking idly.

SAPPHO

Armageddon

*W*e live in an impenitent age; fearing . . . the same sort of
world-catastrophe which our ancestors hoped for.

RONALD A. KNOX

*N*o species is guaranteed its tenure on this planet. And
humans, the first beings to devise the means for their own
destruction, have been here for only several million years.

CARL SAGAN

*W*e are in the 44th year of the Bomb. While it is certainly not
proof, it is nevertheless Exhibit A of the grace of God that this
little planet, Earth, is still here and that we continue our
common lives on it.

JAMES A. SANDERS

*I*n extinction a darkness falls over the world not because the
lights have gone out but because the eyes that behold the light
have been closed.

JONATHAN SCHELL

*I*n the biblical story of Noah, the promise God makes to
humanity is that He will not destroy the world again. For
millennia that promise was a comfort. But for our time it
contains a chilling omission: God does not promise to prevent us
from destroying ourselves.

DAVID WOLPE

Art

*A*rt is a vision of heaven gratuitously given. Being quasi-divine, it is beyond human concerns.

ANTHONY BURGESS

*Y*our art is as it were a grandchild of God.

DANTE

*A*rt is the stored honey of the human soul gathered on wings of misery and travail.

THEODORE DREISER

*M*en continue to be creative in poetry and art only so long as they are religious.

J. W. VON GOETHE

*T*he right hand of the artist withers when he forgets the sovereignty of God.

ABRAHAM JOSHUA HESCHEL

*I*f there were no other proof of the infinite patience of God with men, a very good one could be found in His toleration of the pictures that are painted of Him and of the noise that proceeds from musical instruments under the pretext of being in his "honor."

THOMAS MERTON

Good art is nothing but a replica of the perfection of God and a reflection of His art.

MICHELANGELO

The essential purpose of art, its raison d'être, is to assist in the perfection of the moral personality which is man, and for this reason it must itself be moral.

POPE PIUS XI

Atheism/Agnosticism

*N*o man in a thousand has the strength of mind or goodness of heart to be an atheist.

SAMUEL TAYLOR COLERIDGE

I have never been afflicted by the idea of God. I have never awakened in the middle of the night and said, without the idea of God my life is useless and meaningless.

CLIFTON FADIMAN

*A*theism leads not to badness, but only to an incurable sadness and loneliness.

W. P. MONTAGUE

A skeptical atheism or agnosticism is not necessarily the highest state of understanding at which human beings can arrive. To the contrary, there is reason to believe that behind spurious notions and false concepts of God there lies a reality that is God.

M. SCOTT PECK

*A*theism is the source of all iniquities.

PHILO

*M*y atheism, like that of Spinoza, is true piety towards the universe and denies only gods fashioned by men in their own image, to be servants of their human interests.

GEORGE SANTAYANA

*A*theism can only mean the attempt to remove any ultimate concern—to remain unconcerned about the meaning of one's existence.

PAUL TILLICH

*O*f two men who have no experience of god, he who denies Him is perhaps nearer to Him than the other.

SIMONE WEIL

*A*gnosticism should have its ritual no less than faith. It has sown its martyrs, it should reap its saints, and praise god daily for having hidden Himself from man.

OSCAR WILDE

Beauty

*B*eauty is eternity gazing at itself in a mirror.

KAHLIL GIBRAN

*T*he beautiful is holiness visible, holiness seen, heard, touched, holiness tasted.

ERIC GILL

*B*eauty Eternal came forth from the Holy Places of Mystery to beam on all horizons and all souls and a single ray darting from Her, struck earth and its Heavens; and so she was revealed in the mirror of created things.

MURU'D-DIN ABD-ER-RAHMAN JAMI

*T*he beauty, the grace and the attractiveness of creatures, when compared in their entirety with the beauty of God, are utterly ugly and horrible.

ST. JOHN OF THE CROSS

A soft, smooth, slippery thing, and therefore of a nature which easily slips in and permeates our souls. For I affirm that the good is the beautiful.

PLATO

*T*he beauty that addresses itself to the eyes is only the spell of the moment; the eye of the body is not always that of the soul.

GEORGE SAND

*B*eauty captivates the flesh in order to obtain permission to pass right through to the soul.

SIMONE WEIL

Bible

*C*hurchgoers are used to lukewarm yogurt, but the Bible is about sin, scandal, violence, about lousy authorities, sex, money—what life is about today.

DANIEL BERRIGAN

*W*hat a book! Great and wide as the world rooted in the abysmal depths of creation and rising aloft into the blue mysteries of heaven. . . . sunrise and sunset, promise and fulfillment, birth and death, the whole human drama, everything is in this book. . . . It is the book of books, *Biblia.*

HEINRICH HEINE

*A*ll human history as described in the Bible may be summarized in one phrase. God in Search of Man.

ABRAHAM JOSHUA HESCHEL

*W*hen you are really instructed in the Divine Scriptures, and have realized that its laws and testimonies are the bonds of truth, you can contend with adversaries.

ST. JEROME

*E*verything in the Sacred Books shines and glistens, even in its outer shell: but the marrow of it is sweeter: if you want the kernel, you must break the shell.

ST. JEROME

I think I know which is God's favorite book of the Bible. I think it has to be the Book of Psalms. In the rest of the Bible, God speaks to us—through seers, sages and prophets, through the history of the Israelite people. But in the Psalms we speak to Him.

HAROLD KUSHNER

*W*hat God has so plainly declared to the world is in some parts of scripture stated in plain words, while in other parts it still lies hidden under obscure words.

MARTIN LUTHER

*T*he Old Testament is responsible for more atheism, agnosticism, disbelief—call it what you will—than any book every written; it has emptied more churches than all the counterattractions of cinema, motor bicycle and golf course.

A. A. MILNE

*W*hen you eat fish, you don't eat the bones. You eat the flesh. Take the Bible like that.

ROBERT LEE MORTON

I do not call you 'back to the Bible.' I urge you to run hard enough and fast enough to catch up with the Bible.

JAMES A. SANDERS

*T*he devil can cite Scripture for his purpose.

WILLIAM SHAKESPEARE

I am a Bible-bigot. I follow it in all things, both great and small.

JOHN WESLEY

Body & Mind

These bodies are perishable; but the dwellers in these bodies are eternal, indestructible, and impenetrable.

BHAGAVAD-GITA

Your business is to find the real nature of the mind. Then you find there is no mind. When the Self is sought the mind is not.

PAUL BRUNTON

When camphor burns no residue is left. The mind is the camphor, when it has resolved itself into the self without leaving the slightest trace it is Realisation.

PAUL BRUNTON

It is good to tame the mind; which is difficult to hold in and flighty, rushing wherewith it listeth; a tamed mind brings happiness.

DHAMMAPADA

He who knows that this body is like froth, and has learnt that it is as unsubstantial as a mirage, will break the flower-pointed arrow of Mara, and never see the king of death.

DHAMMAPADA

*I*f only you could suddenly be unaware of all things, then you could pass into an oblivion of your own body.

MEISTER ECKHART

*O*f the universal mind each individual man is one more incarnation.

RALPH WALDO EMERSON

*M*ind is the master. What hasn't been created by thought doesn't exist.

AYYA KEMMA

*M*y great religion is a belief in the blood, the flesh, as being wiser than the intellect. We can go wrong in our minds. But what our blood feels and believes and says, is always true.

D. H. LAWRENCE

*T*he body is a vessel which He wrought, and into which He infused His workmanship and skill.

NĀNAK

*T*he mind, which sometimes presumes to believe that there is no such thing as a miracle, is itself a miracle.

M. SCOTT PECK

*T*he body is the tomb of the soul.

PLATO

Buddha

The Buddha and all his successors warn us against intellectual structures that confine us to an artificial environment, and against concepts that smear over the living fact of things in themselves.

ROBERT AITKEN

I will not accept the Buddhahood if all who, with sincere faith, desire to be reborn in my Paradise are not to enter it. If all men save deadly sinners may not enter it, I will not enter Buddhahood.

BODDHISATTVA AMITABHA

In Zen enlightenment, the discovery of the "original face before you were born" is the discovery not that one *sees* Buddha but that one *is* Buddha.

THOMAS MERTON

The Buddha came to save the world, and his method for the accomplishment of this end is the destruction of ignorance and the dissemination of knowledge as to the true values of life and the wise way to live. The Buddha indeed cannot save us; we must do that for ourselves . . . in large part through the attainment and application of his knowledge or insight.

J. D. PRATT

*I*f the Element of the Buddha did not exist [in everyone] there could be no disgust with suffering.

RATNA-GOTRA-VIBHAGA

*I*f all beings are Buddha, why all this striving?

DOGEN ZENJI

Buddhism

*M*oreover, brethren, though robbers, who are highwaymen, would with a two-handed saw carve you in pieces limb by limb, yet if the mind of any one of you should be offended thereat, such a one is no follower of my gospel.

BUDDHA

I came away from my joust with Zen bruised, humbled, and, I hope, a little wiser. I also came away knowing that I had touched the outer edge of something *other* than anything I had ever known before.

HARVEY COX

*T*he sermon on the Mount has (and very justly I believe) been compared to Zen in that it describes the undifferentiated consciousness of one who lives in the here-and-now with joy and without care.

WILLIAM JOHNSTON

*W*e come now to the very heart of Zen, which is, it might be said, to commit spiritual suicide.

KENNETH KRAMER

*Z*en pushes contradictions to their ultimate limit where one has to choose between madness and innocence.

THOMAS MERTON

*I*n Zen practice, to gain is to lose, to lose is to gain. To let everything go is to gain it all.

DAVID MERZEL

*I*n Buddhism, being cannot strictly be predicated of any thing, or of any god or animal or man—each is really only becoming.

SACRED BOOKS OF THE EAST

*B*uddhism has tried to quiet a sick world with anesthetics; Christianity sought to purge it with fire.

GEORGE SANTAYANA

*T*he ultimate standpoint of Zen . . . is that we have been led astray through ignorance to find a split in our own being, that there was from the very beginning no need for a struggle between the finite and the infinite, that the peace we are seeking so eagerly after has been there all the time.

D. T. SUZUKI

*B*uddhism is negative. It will tell you what it is not. When you insist that it must be something it merely allows for an open space, which you can fill in as you like.

JANWILLEM VAN DE WETERING

Catholicism

You are not to be looked upon as holding the true Catholic Faith if you do not teach that the faith of Rome is to be held.

ST. AUGUSTINE

The most important thing about me is that I am a Catholic. It's a superstructure within which to work, like a sonnet.

JEAN KERR

The Vatican rejects the pick-and-choose kind of K-mart Catholicism so prevalent in the United States. It is telling the bishops their job is to communicate the real things, not fashionable counterfeits.

JOHN NAVONE

Modern Catholicism is nothing else but simply the legitimate growth and complement, that is, the natural and necessary development of the doctrine of the early Church.

JOHN HENRY NEWMAN

Celibacy & Sexuality

*A*n advance beyond moderation in demanding the due of either sex . . . is allowed to married persons as a matter of pardon.

ST. AUGUSTINE

*S*ex which is not integrated and transfigured by spirit is always evidence of man's subjugation to the genus.

NIKOLAY BERDYAYEV

*A*s rain breaks through an ill-thatched roof, so lust breaks through an ill-trained mind.

DHAMMAPADA

*L*onging for physical union with someone indicates the urge to return home, to rejoin the one time consciousness. It is said in Taoism that living in the world, we are like a small river returning home.

DHIRAVAMSA

*C*hastity is the cement of civilization and progress.

MARY BAKER EDDY

*J*udaism does not regard sexual union as a concession to the flesh but as a proper and sacred act.

ARTHUR HERTZBERG

*S*exual expression generates more energy for passionate involvement in the movements for justice in the world. Lovemaking turns us simultaneously *into* ourselves and *beyond* ourselves.

CARTER HEYWARD

*N*othing is better than a celibate life.

HORACE

*I*f anyone is able to abide in chastity to the honor of the flesh of our Lord, let him so abide without boasting.

ST. IGNATIUS OF ANTIOCH

*S*exuality is in fact a privileged area for a Christian life according to the Spirit of freedom. . . . When we allow the Spirit to lead us we are saying in effect that we do not let ourselves be led blindly by our instincts but, rather, place these at the service of genuine love.

BAKOLE WA ILUNGA

*T*o the extent that [celibate people] bear effective witness, in and through their celibacy, to a life that is full, free, and happy, they are a living challenge to a mentality and a society that regard sexuality as an absolute value and the key to all happiness and that judge a woman by her physical charms or a man by his sexual prowess.

BAKOLE WA ILUNGA

*T*he Law is my pond, celibacy is my bathing place, which is not turbid, and throughout clear for the soul; therein make ablutions; pure, clean and thoroughly cooled, I get rid of hatred (or impurity).

JAINA SUTRAS

*M*arriage has many pains but celibacy no pleasures.

SAMUEL JOHNSON

*E*ros, honoured without reservation and obeyed unconditionally, becomes a demon.

SAMUEL JOHNSON

*W*hoever cannot bridle his carnal affections, let him keep them without the bounds of lawful wedlock.

LACTANTIUS

*T*he state of celibacy is great hypocrisy and wickedness. Christ with one sentence confutes all their arguments: God created them male and female.

MARTIN LUTHER

*O*ne of the greatest mistakes of Christian thinking through the centuries has been that sharp separation so many theologians and spiritual guides have made between 'love carnal' and 'love seraphic.' There are really no sharp lines of distinction between 'sacred' and 'profane' love.

JOSEPH NEEDHAM

*W*e should not expect . . . to be able to block out our sexual feelings without blocking out the longing for social relations rooted in mutuality rather than hierarchy, without blocking out the anger that warns us that something is amiss in our present social arrangements, without blocking and distorting the fullness of our love for God.

JUDITH PLASKOW

*W*e have two tyrannous physical passions: concupiscence and chastity. We become mad in pursuit of sex: we become equally mad in the persecution of that pursuit. Unless we gratify our desire the race is lost; unless we restrain it we destroy ourselves.

GEORGE BERNARD SHAW

*L*ove and sex are the things that give life some value, some zest. Miserable as flesh and blood is, it is still the best you can get.

ISAAC BASHEVIS SINGER

*C*hastity is a wealth that comes from abundance of love.

RABINDRANATH TAGORE

*S*alvation, in the case of men as well as of women, depends chiefly on the observance of chastity.

TERTULLIAN

*I*t is lust, not the act itself, that makes sexual union shameful; it is excess, not the [marital] state as such, that is unchaste.

TERTULLIAN

Charity

*G*iving alms never lessens the purse.

AFRICAN PROVERB

*T*hat money will be more profitable to you . . . if you so give it
to a poor man that you actually bestow it on Christ.

ST. AMBROSE

*T*he chill of charity is the silence of the heart: the flame of
charity is the clamor of the heart.

ST. AUGUSTINE

A disciple having asked for a definition of charity, the Master
said LOVE ONE ANOTHER.

CONFUCIUS

*F*or it is to the humanity in a man that we give, and not to his
moral character.

JULIAN THE APOSTATE

*W*e live in the century of the Appeal. . . . One applauds the
industry of professional philanthropy. But it has its dangers.
After a while the private heart begins to harden. We fling
letters into the wastebasket, are abrupt to telephone
solicitations. Charity withers in the incessant gale.

PHYLLIS MCGINLEY

*T*here are eight rungs in charity. The highest is when you help a man to help himself.

MOSES MAIMONIDES

*B*read for myself is a material question; bread for my neighbor is a spiritual question.

JACQUES MARITAIN

*T*he dramatic Christianity of the organ and aisle, of dawn-service and twilight revival . . . this gaslighted, and gas-inspired Christianity, we are triumphant in. . . . You had better get rid of the smoke, and the organ pipes . . . and the Gothic windows and the painted glass . . . and look after Lazarus at the doorstep.

JOHN RUSKIN

*C*harity never humiliated him who profiteth from it, nor ever bound him by the chains of gratitude, since it was not to him but to God that the gift was made.

ANTOINE DE SAINT-EXUPÉRY

*C*are of the poor is incumbent on society as a whole.

BARUCH SPINOZA

*C*harity, to be fruitful, must cost us.

MOTHER TERESA

*C*harity. To love human beings insofar as they are nothing. That is to love them as God does.

SIMONE WEIL

Children

Blessed be childhood, which brings down something of heaven into the midst of our rough earthliness.

HENRI FREDERIC AMIEL

But the child's sob in the silence curses deeper
Than the strong man in his wrath.

ELIZABETH BARRETT BROWNING

Your children are not your children. They are the sons and daughters of Life's longing for itself.

KAHLIL GIBRAN

A child's mind is, indeed, throughout the best clue to understanding of savage magic. A young and vital child knows no limit to his own will, and it is the only reality to him. It is not that he wants at the outset to fight other wills, but that they simply do not exist for him. Like the artist, he goes forth to the work of creation, gloriously alone.

JANE ELLEN HARRISON

The sublimest song to be heard on earth is the lisping of the human soul on the lips of children.

VICTOR HUGO

*C*hildren, who are closer to their birth and thus to the experience of Oneness, rightly reject hypocrisy.

VIMALIA McCLURE

*I*f help and salvation are to come, they can only come from the children, for the children are the makers of men.

MARIA MONTESSORI

*E*very child comes with the message that God is not yet discouraged of man.

RABINDRANATH TAGORE

Christianity

*W*ith the rise of Christianity, faith replaced thought as the bringer of immortality.

HANNAH ARENDT

*B*ecause [Christians] acknowledge the goodness of God towards them, lo! on account of them there flows forth the beauty that is in the world.

ARISTIDES

*I*t is not some religious set that makes a Christian what he is, but participation in the suffering of God in the light of the world.

DIETRICH BONHOEFFER

*T*he Christian must plunge himself into the life of the godless world without attempting to gloss over its ungodliness with a veneer of religion, or trying to transfigure it. He must live a "worldly" life and so participate in the suffering God.

DIETRICH BONHOEFFER

[*C*hristians] are a secret tribe that lurks in darkness and shuns the light, silent in public, chattering in corners.

CAECILIUS

*C*hristianity has compelled the mind of man not because it is the most cheering view of man's existence but because it is truest to the facts.

DAVID CECIL

*C*hristianity is always out of fashion because it is always sane; and all fashions are mild insanities.

G. K. CHESTERTON

*C*hristians are left with the 'stubborn, irreducible fact' that our faith is centered on a Jew. The shortest way to describe Christians is that we are Gentiles who try to serve and worship the God of the Jews.

HARVEY COX

*T*hat a few simple men should in one generation have invented so powerful and appealing a personality, so lofty an ethic and so inspiring a vision of human brotherhood, would be a miracle far more incredible than any recorded in the Gospel.

WILL DURANT

*W*e cannot pretend that life in Christ always means victory, miracle and success in this life. When we tell only the stories of victory, we tell only a part of the truth. When we recount only the answered prayers, we oversimplify. When we imply the Christian faith involves no yoke, we lie.

BILLY GRAHAM

*O*ne must either resolutely deny, combat and persecute Christianity, or one must really live it. What lies between is the cult of genius and deceit.

SØREN KIERKEGAARD

*T*here is a deeper sense of the word "Christian" in which some who hold wrong beliefs may be more Christian than some who hold the right ones.

C. S. LEWIS

A Christian is not he that hath no sin, or feeleth no sin, but to whom God imputeth not his sin because of his faith in Christ.

MARTIN LUTHER

*I*t is one thing to say that men are free to believe what they choose, and another thing to say that it is all right for them to call anything the choose to believe "Christianity." Matters of fact are at stake here.

JAMES A. MARTIN, JR.

*C*hristianity must now rise above the limitations of orthodoxy just as the free world must rise above the limitations of nationalism if we are not to pull the civilized world down around our ears.

AGNES MEYER

*T*he whole course of Christianity from the first, when we come to examine it, is but one series of troubles and disorders.

JOHN HENRY NEWMAN

*C*hristianity came to the nations as a beam of light shot into chaos; a strain of sweet music—so silvery and soft we know not we are listening—to him who wanders on amid the uncertain gloom, and charms him to the light, to the River of God and tree of Life.

THEODORE PARKER

No one can say that Christianity has failed. It has never been tried.

ADAM CLAYTON POWELL

I do not mean that Christianity is over. I mean that society is not going to be influenced by it as it was before. We may be apt to despair at this, but history shows that Christianity undergoes a great crisis every 500 years or so, dying to be reborn.

FULTON SHEEN

One has even reached a point today where some Christians can speak of believing in Christianity (instead of believing in God and Christ); of preaching Christianity (instead of preaching good news, salvation, redemption); of practicing Christianity (instead of practicing love).

WILFRED C. SMITH

Going to church doesn't make a man a Christian any more than going to a garage makes him an automobile.

BILLY SUNDAY

Away with all attempts to produce a Stoic, Platonic, and dialectic Christianity! We want no curious disputation after possessing Jesus Christ, no inquisition after receiving the gospel!

TERTULLIAN

It is the maturest fruit of Christian understanding to understand that Christianity, as such, is of no avail.

PAUL TILLICH

*C*hristianity places our conduct in this life on earth in its gigantic setting of infinity and eternity, and by opening our eyes to this vast spiritual vision it calls out our deepest spiritual energies.

ARNOLD J. TOYNBEE

*W*hat makes Christ's teachings difficult is that they obligate us to do something about them.

JOHN J. WADE

*T*o make Christianity conform fully to the modern rational mood, it would have to cease to be Christianity.

BARBARA WARD

Church

The Church is like the ark of Noah, outside of which nobody can be saved.

ST. THOMAS AQUINAS

The Church has succumbed to the temptation to believe in the goodness and power of her own tradition, morality and religious activity. So the Church has come to believe in images of man, of the world, and of God which she has fabricated of her own means.

KARL BARTH

Everyday people are straying away from the church and going back to God. Really.

LENNY BRUCE

The greatest failure of the church and synagogue may be that we are too "unexpectant." We have become so enamored with secular interpretations of things that we do not expect and anticipate the power that can come through God.

ERNEST CAMPBELL

The role of the church is to be the conscience of the society, not provide the solution for its problems.

STERLING CARY

I endure the church till the day I see a better one.

DESIDERIUS ERASMUS

I look forward with great anticipation to the death of the church. The sooner it dies, the sooner we can be about the business of living the gospel.

SALLY GEARHART

If we had more hell in the pulpit, we would have less hell in the pew.

BILLY GRAHAM

We do not want churches because they will teach us to quarrel about God.

CHIEF JOSEPH

The church must be reminded that it is not the master or the servant of the state, but rather the conscience of the state. It must be the guide and critic of the state, and never its tool. If the church does not recapture its prophetic zeal, it will become an irrelevant social club without moral or spiritual authority.

MARTIN LUTHER KING, JR.

In our times it is not secularism but do-it-yourself religion that is the real enemy of the church.

MARTIN E. MARTY

My own mind is my own church.

THOMAS PAINE

Sometimes I get the sense that what will destroy the church is going to be not persecution but boredom.

JAROSLAV PELIKAN

The male church has never understood that the reality of the Church is based on the shared humanity of man and woman.

UTA RANKE-HEINEMANN

Churches don't need new members half so much as they need the old bunch made over.

BILLY SUNDAY

The self-preserving church is in the process of suicide.

GARDNER C. TAYLOR

Clergy

I don't believe women can be priests any more than they can be fathers or husbands.

JOHN M. ALLIN

*J*esus never intended to narrow ministry to priests; nor did He ever intend to do what we have done, namely to narrow priests down to highly educated, middle- and upper-class, white male celibates.

FRANK BONNIKE

*T*he bishops will govern the Church, the priests will do all the work and the deacons will have all the fun.

RICHARD CARDINAL CUSHING

*P*eople expect the clergy to have the grace of a swan, the friendliness of a sparrow, the strength of an eagle and the night hours of an owl—and some people expect such a bird to live on the food of a canary.

EDWARD JEFFREY

*T*he most effective way to serve God is still the method practiced by Christ Jesus and the Prophet Muhammed. They both were roving preachers.

WALLACE DEAN MUHAMMED

The pulpit calls those anointed to it as the sea calls its sailors, and, like the sea, it batters and bruises, and does not rest.

BRUCE THIELEMANN

There is something uniquely valuable that women and men bring to the ordained ministry, and it has been distorted and defective as long as women have been debarred. Somehow men have been less human for this loss.

DESMOND TUTU

The clergy have lost their hold. In America a man in trouble now goes to his doctor.

ALFRED NORTH WHITEHEAD

If you dismiss them from the priesthood simply because they are female, they can do nothing because God Almighty made them that way. By questioning their admission to the priesthood because they are women, you are questioning the judgment of God Almighty.

CHARLES WILLIE

Community & Fellowship

I believe we are placed here to be companions—a wonderful word that comes from *cum panis* ("with bread"). We are here to share bread with one another so that everyone has enough, no one has too much and our social order achieves this goal with maximal freedom and minimal coercion.

ROBERT MCAFEE BROWN

*W*e can build a community out of seekers of truth, but not out of possessors of truth.

WILLIAM SLOANE COFFIN

*W*e have merely to assert what already exists deep within us—namely a sense of kinship.

NORMAN COUSINS

*W*e are born in relation, we live in relation, we die in relation. There is, literally, no such human place as simply "inside myself." Nor is any person, creed, ideology, or movement entirely "outside myself."

CARTER HEYWARD

*W*ithout the witness of human beings, there might as well be no God. God requires a community of belief and attestation.

BARRY HOLTZ

*I*t is as we join with others, in a way that only human beings can, in shared engagement to a common vision, that we find ourselves in the presence of another presence that is the final source of our hopes and intentions, and that undergirds and sustains them.

JUDITH PLASKOW

*A*ll the functions of church—the repentance by which we enter it, the Eucharist by which we commune with it, and the ministry by which we mutually empower it—are simply expressions of entering and developing a true human community of mutual love.

ROSEMARY RADFORD RUETHER

*W*e witness . . . by being a community of reconciliation, a forgiving community of the forgiven.

DESMOND TUTU

Compassion

Compassion is the chief law of human existence.

FYODOR DOSTOYEVSKY

There can be no compassion without celebration. Compassion operates at the same level as celebration because what is of most moment in compassion is not feelings of pity but feelings of togetherness.

MATTHEW FOX

God created a reminder, an image. Humanity is a reminder of God. As God is compassionate, let humanity be compassionate.

ABRAHAM JOSHUA HESCHEL

The whole idea of compassion is based on a keen awareness of the interdependence of all these living beings, which are all part of one another, and all involved in one another.

THOMAS MERTON

There is no wilderness so terrible, so beautiful, so arid, so fruitful, as the wilderness of compassion. It is the only desert that shall truly flourish like a lily.

THOMAS MERTON

What value has compassion that does not take its object in its arms.

ANTOINE DE SAINT-EXUPÉRY

Conduct

*L*ive by the commandments. Do not die by them.

BABYLONIAN TALMUD

*L*et the superior man never fail reverently to order his own conduct, and let him be respectful to others, and observant of property—then all within the four seas will be his brothers.

CONFUCIUS

A man of humanity is one who, in seeking to establish himself, finds a foothold for others and who, desiring attainment for himself, helps others to attain.

CONFUCIUS

A real Christian is a person who can give his pet parrot to a town gossip.

BILLY GRAHAM

*W*hat is hateful to you do not do to another. This is the whole of the Law, the rest is Commentary. Go, learn the commentary.

HILLEL

The only general persuasive in matters of conduct is authority; that is (when truth is in question), a judgment which we feel to be superior to our own.

JOHN HENRY NEWMAN

Live with men as if God saw you; converse with God as if men heard you.

SENECA

Conscience

Conscience is the perfect interpreter of life.

KARL BARTH

Conscience is thoroughly well bred and soon leaves off talking to those who do not wish to hear it.

SAMUEL BUTLER

No man serves God with a good conscience, who serves him against his reason.

SAMUEL TAYLOR COLERIDGE

Yet while conscience thus insists we do right, it does not by itself tell us what is right.

HARRY EMERSON FOSDICK

We fluctuate long between love and hatred before we can arrive at tranquility.

HÉLOISE

The conscious person is continuous with a wider self through which saving experiences come.

WILLIAM JAMES

God's law enters our mind and draws it to itself by stirring up conscience, which itself is called the law of our mind.

ST. JOHN DAMASCENE

Men will never do evil so fully and so happily as when they do it for conscience's sake.

BLAISE PASCAL

There is no witness so terrible, no accuser so potent, as the conscience that dwells in every man's breast.

POLYBIUS

A peace above all earthly dignities,
A still and quiet conscience.

WILLIAM SHAKESPEARE

Christianity can never be a merely personal matter. It has public consequences, and we must make public choices.

DESMOND TUTU

Contentment & Happiness

*H*appiness is like a cat. If you try to coax it or call it, it will avoid you; it will never come. But if you pay no attention to it and go about your business, you'll find it rubbing against your legs and jumping into your lap.

WILLIAM BENNETT

*T*he supreme happiness of life is the conviction that we are loved.

VICTOR HUGO

*T*he first requisite for the happiness of the people is the abolition of religion.

KARL MARX

*T*o accept what you are is to be content, and contentment is the greatest wealth. To work with patience is to gather power. To surrender to the Eternal flow is to be completely present.

VIMALIA MCCLURE

*T*he Vision of God is the greatest happiness to which man can attain. . . . Our imprisonment in bodies of clay and water and entanglement in the things of sense constitute a veil which hides the Vision of God from us.

ABU-HĀMID MUHAMMAD AL-GHAZĀLĪ

*G*od, give us grace to accept with serenity the things that cannot be changed, courage to change the things that should be changed and the wisdom to distinguish the one from the other.

REINHOLD NIEBUHR

*K*nowledge of Him is the consummation of happiness.

PHILO OF ALEXANDRIA

*O*ur Savior has nowhere promised to make us infallibly happy in this world.

POPE PIUS XI

I have lived long enough myself to know that loss and sorrow are what we must expect as our portion in this life. If happiness comes in, it is only by the way.

MURASAKI SHIKIBU

*O*f no mortal say "That man is happy," till vexed by no grievous ill he pass Life's goal.

SOPHOCLES

*H*appiness is an imaginary condition, formerly attributed by the living to the dead, now usually attributed by adults to children, and by children to adults.

THOMAS SZASZ

*H*oliness is a greater ideal by far than happiness because it embraces struggle and sees all things—achievement, aspiration, even love—as part of the moral drama of the world and not as life's end or sole reason for being.

DAVID WOLPE

Conversion

Conversion has to materialize in small actions as well as in great.

ROBERT HUGH BENSON

You come to God in many ways. A student I knew read the Summa of Thomas Aquinas, said "that's it," threw up his career, changed his religion and became a priest. Julian of Norwich, in the Middle Ages, had a bad dose of flu, ran a temperature and saw visions.

LIONEL BLUE

Evangelical conversion is indeed the touchstone of all spirituality. Conversion means a radical transformation of ourselves; it means thinking, feeling, and living as Christ—present in exploited and alienated man.

GUSTAVO GUTIERREZ

Compulsion in religion is distinguished peculiarly from compulsion in every other thing. I may grow rich by an art I am compelled to follow; I may recover health by medicines I am compelled to take against my own judgment; but I cannot be saved by a worship I disbelieve and abhor.

THOMAS JEFFERSON

*P*eople who think that once they are converted all will be happy, have forgotten Satan.

MARTYN LLOYD-JONES

*Y*ou have not converted a man because you have silenced him.

JOHN MORLEY

*M*en often mistake their imagination for the promptings of their heart and believe they are converted the moment they think of conversion.

BLAISE PASCAL

*L*et there be no compulsion in religion.

QUR'ĀN

I think I am the only person who was actually converted at his own confirmation service.

ROBERT RUNCIE

*K*indness has converted more people than zeal, science or eloquence.

MOTHER TERESA

Courage

*C*ourage is rightly esteemed the first of human qualities, because . . . it is the quality that guarantees all others.

WINSTON CHURCHILL

*C*ourage is the price that Life exacts for granting peace.

AMELIA EARHART

*O*n Calvary there was one man brave enough to die and one woman brave enough to go on living; so all men may know that life and death demand the same ingredient of courage.

WALTER FARRELL

*C*ourage calls to courage everywhere, and its voice cannot be denied.

MILLICENT GARRET FAWCETT

*W*e worship God not because He will make our path smooth, but because He gives us the grace and determination to keep walking even when the path is rocky.

HAROLD KUSHNER

*L*ife shrinks or expands in proportion to one's courage.

ANAÏS NIN

*O*ne thinks like a hero to behave like a merely decent human being.

MAY SARTON

Creation

*T*o suppose that God formed man from the dust with bodily hands is very childish . . . God neither formed man with bodily hands nor did he breathe upon him with throat and lips.

ST. AUGUSTINE

*I*t is easier to think of the world without a creator than of a creator loaded with all the contradictions of the world.

SIMONE DE BEAUVOIR

*T*he doctrine of creation is not a speculative cosmogony, but a confession of faith, of faith in God as Lord.

RUDOLF BULTMANN

*D*ivinity is not playful. The universe was not made in jest but in solemn incomprehensible earnest. By a power that is unfathomably secret, and holy, and fleet. There is nothing to be done about it, but ignore it, or see.

ANNIE DILLARD

*W*hat really interests me is whether God had any choice in the creation of the world.

ALBERT EINSTEIN

*A*ll of creation is a song of praise to God.

HILDEGARD OF BINGEN

*T*his universe existed in the shape of Darkness, unperceived
. . . the divine appeared with irresistible creative power,
dispelling the darkness.

MANU-SMRITI

*T*he creation is the Bible of the Deist. He there reads in the
handwriting of the Creator himself, the certainty of his
existence, and the immutability of his power.

THOMAS PAINE

*G*od is really only another artist. He invented the elephant, the
giraffe and the cat. He has no real style. He just goes on trying
other things.

PABLO PICASSO

*T*he characteristic common to God and man is apparently
. . . the desire and the ability to make things.

DOROTHY SAYERS

*W*e were intellectually intoxicated with the idea that the world
could make itself without design, purpose, skill or intelligence;
in short, without life.

GEORGE BERNARD SHAW

*T*he event of creation did not take place so many kalpas or aeons
ago, astronomically or biologically speaking. Creation is taking
place every moment of our lives.

D. T. SUZUKI

*T*o assert that a world as intricate as ours emerged from chaos by chance is about as sensible as to claim that Shakespeare's dramas were composed by rioting monkeys in a print shop.

MERRILL C. TENNEY

*C*reation by the Word out of nothing describes the absolute independence of God as creator, the absolute dependence of creation, and the infinite gap between.

PAUL TILLICH

Crucifixion & Resurrection

*I*f it has to choose who is to be crucified, the crowd will always save Barabbas.

JEAN COCTEAU

*J*esus' death on the cross represented God's boundless solidarity with victims, even unto death.

JAMES CONE

*T*he cross is the ladder to heaven.

THOMAS DRAXE

*T*he cross preceded the resurrection; but the resurrection has not abolished the cross. Suffering, sin, betrayal, cruelty of every kind, continued to exist after the crucifixion, and they continue still. This is the failure of the cross. God made failure an instrument of victory.

UNA KROLL

*T*he cross epitomizes the retribution that comes to those who give up controlling and triumphalist postures in order to relate to others in mutual love.

SALLIE MCFAGUE

The Cross is where history and life, legend and reality, time and eternity, intersect. There, Jesus is nailed forever to show us how God would become a man and a man become God.

MALCOLM MUGGERIDGE

Without the Resurrection, Good Friday would only be the triumph of evil.

MAURICE NEDONCELLE

The only shadow that the Cross casts over history is one of shelter and asylum.

AMOS WILDER

Death

O son of the Infinite! I made death for thee as glad tidings. Why grievest thou over it? I made light for thee as guidance. Why dost thou hide from it?

BAHAULLAH

*E*very moment of life is the last, every poem is a death poem.

BASHŌ

*T*here is no such thing as a natural death . . . for every man his death is an accident and, even if he knows it and consents to it, an unjustifiable violation.

SIMONE DE BEAUVOIR

*D*eath will come, always out of season.

CHIEF BIG ELK

*T*he first sign of love to God is not to be afraid of death and to be always waiting for it. For death unites the friend to his friend—the seeker to the object which he seeks.

ABU-HĀMID MUHAMMAD AL-GHAZĀLĪ

The meaning of death is not the annihilation of the spirit, but its separation from the body, and that the resurrection and day of assembly do not mean a return to a new existence after annihilation, but the bestowal of a new form or frame to the spirit.

ABU-HĀMID MUHAMMAD AL-GHAZĀLĪ

When a man dies they who survive him ask what property he has left behind: The angel who bends over the dying man asks what good deeds he has sent before him.

QUR'ĀN

Unlike life, death cannot be taken away from man, and therefore we may consider it as *the* gift of God.

SENECA

That day, which you fear as being the end of all things, is the birthday of your eternity.

SENECA

Peace, Peace! He is not dead, he doth not sleep—
He hath awakened from the dream of life.

PERCY BYSSHE SHELLEY

If you live wrong you can't die right.

BILLY SUNDAY

Though lovers be lost love shall not,
and death shall have no dominion.

DYLAN THOMAS

One who knows the Self puts death to death.

UPANISHADS

It's no comfort to know that one life follows another and is itself the prelude to a new life. Life continues and with it fear. Fear of death, fear of birth. Real, definite death would be more of a comfort.

JANWILLEM VAN DE WETERING

Desire

*T*hat man attains peace who, abandoning all desires, moves about without attachment and longing, without the sense of "I" and "mine."

BHAGAVAD-GITA

*I*t is by that which he longs for, that every man knows and apprehends the quality with which he has to serve God.

MARTIN BUBER

*C*ut down the whole forest of desire, not just one tree only.

DHAMMAPADA

*E*very desire is a viper in the bosom, who, while he was chilled was harmless; but when warmth gave him strength, exerted its poison.

SAMUEL JOHNSON

*C*raving is the hankering after pleasure, or existence, or success. It is the germ from which springs all human misery.

VINAYA, MAHAVAGGA

*I*f we go down into ourselves we find that we possess exactly what we desire.

SIMONE WEIL

Despair

Despair is the conclusion of fools.

BENJAMIN DISRAELI

Do not abandon yourself to despair. We are the Easter people and Hallelujah is our song.

POPE JOHN PAUL II

When the sinner despairs of the forgiveness of sin, it is almost as if he were directly picking a quarrel with God.

SØREN KIERKEGAARD

If there is no God, and everything, therefore, is permitted, the first thing permitted is despair.

FRANÇOIS MAURIAC

If Religion was not needed to keep bad men in check, it still would be needed to keep good men from despair.

OLD FARMER'S ALMANAC

Despair [is] the rejection of God within oneself.

ANTOINE DE SAINT-EXUPÉRY

Detachment

The man who, casting off all desires, lives free from attachment; who is free from egoism and from the feeling that this or that is mine, obtains tranquility.

BHAGAVAD-GITA

Let, therefore, no man love anything; loss of the beloved is evil. Those who love nothing, and hate nothing, have no fetters.

DHAMMAPADA

A sound heart can turn away any situation in which it is placed without resistance or suffering, if it is not pulled by or attached to that situation.

SHAYKH FADHLELLA HAERI

Detachment, the foundation of all mystic techniques, may be compressed into the formula: I will not to will.

ARTHUR KOESTLER

If one is passionately attached to the delights of this world, be they possessions or children, tragedy, even death can sweep them away.

KENNETH KRAMER

Detachment is not a denial of life but a denial of death; not a disintegration but the condition of wholeness; not a refusal to love but the determination to love truly, deeply and fully.

GERALD VANN

Determinism & Free Will

*D*estiny, n.   A tyrant's authority for crime and a fool's excuse for failure.

AMBROSE BIERCE

*L*ife and Death, existence and non-existence, success and non-success, poverty and wealth, virtue and vice, good and evil, hunger and thirst, warmth and cold, all revolve upon the changing wheel of Destiny.

CHUANG-TZU

I call on heaven and earth to witness against you this day, that I have set before you life and death, the blessing and the curse; therefore choose life, that you and your descendants may live, loving the Lord your God, obeying this voice, and cleaving to him, for that is your life and the length of your days.

DEUTERONOMY 30:19–20

*A*t any rate, I am convinced that he [God] does not play dice.

ALBERT EINSTEIN

*Y*ou may fetter my leg, but my will not even Zeus can overpower.

EPICTETUS

God has a peculiar right over the hearts of great men. He has created. When He pleases to touch them He ravishes them and lets them not speak nor breathe but for His glory.

HÉLOISE

To rule by fettering the mind through fear of punishment in another world is just as base as to use force.

HYPATIA

All theory is against the freedom of the will; all experience for it.

SAMUEL JOHNSON

With man degraded to a bundle of conditioned reflexes . . . there remained only an aimless and turbulent moral relativity. . . . This denial of the human soul was the perfect preparation for the revival of tyranny.

WALTER LIPPMANN

When the cards are dealt and you pick up your hand, that is determinism; there's nothing you can do except to play it out for whatever it may be worth. And the way you play your hand is free will.

JAWAHARLAL NEHRU

There is no free will in the human mind: it is moved to this or that volition by some cause, and that cause has been determined by some other cause, and so on infinitely.

BARUCH SPINOZA

Devil

*W*hat is the devil, after all? Just my own weakness, my own lack of courage, the problems I can't face, the bit of my own self I can't love. We are our own devils.

LIONEL BLUE

*T*he devil has power to suggest evil, but he was not given the power to compel you against your will.

ST. CYRIL OF JERUSALEM

I think if the devil doesn't exist, but man has created him, he has created him in his own image and likeness.

FYODOR DOSTOYEVSKY

*I*f one believes in the truth of the Bible, it is impossible to doubt the reality of the Devil for a single moment.

DENIS DE ROUGEMONT

I know there is a devil for two reasons: first, the Bible declares it; and second I have done business with him.

BILLY SUNDAY

*I*n divers way the devil has shown hostility to the Truth. At times he has tried to shake it by pretending to defend it.

TERTULLIAN

The Devil cannot penetrate our intellects to make us reason crookedly, but can fire our imagination and arouse our passions to such an enjoyable degree that we do not wish to use our intellects.

GERALD C. TREACY

Doctrine & Dogma

Doctrine is nothing but the skin of truth, set up and stuffed.

HENRY WARD BEECHER

A doctrine which is but a doctrine has a poor chance indeed of giving birth to the glowing enthusiasm, the illumination, the faith that moves mountains.

HENRI BERGSON

Truths turn into dogmas the moment they are disputed.

G. K. CHESTERTON

As men's prayers are a disease of the will, so are their creeds a disease of the intellect.

RALPH WALDO EMERSON

It would be well if we thought less of our dogmas and more of the gospel.

DESIDERIUS ERASMUS

A religion without dogma is like a parcel tied up without string.

CHRISTINE LONGFORD

No doctrine is defined until it is violated.

JOHN HENRY NEWMAN

What is dogma to the ordinary man is experience to the pure in heart.

SAVREPALLI RADHAKRISHNAN

So long as man quarrels and disputes about doctrines and dogmas, he has not tasted the nectar of true faith; when he has tasted it, he becomes quiet and full of peace.

SRI RAMAKRISHNA

A creed put forward by authority deserves respect in the measure that we respect the authority's claim to be a judge of truth. If the creed and the authority alike are conceived as being arbitrary, capricious, and irrational, we shall continue in a state of terror and bewilderment, since we shall never know from one minute to the next what we are supposed to be doing, or why, or what we have to expect.

DOROTHY SAYERS

No doctrine, however high, however true, can make men happy until it is translated into life.

HENRY VAN DYKE

Doubt

*T*he first key to wisdom is assiduous and frequent questioning.
. . . For by doubting we come to inquiry, and by inquiry we
arrive at the truth.

PETER ABELARD

*N*ever be afraid to doubt, if only you have the disposition to
believe, and doubt in order that you may end in believing
the truth.

SAMUEL TAYLOR COLERIDGE

*F*or he who doubts is like a wave of the sea that is driven and
tossed by the wind.

JAMES 1:6

*H*e that is ever doubting is like the flood of the sea which is
moved and borne about with the wind, and that man is not
likely to receive the gifts of God.

MARGERY KEMPE

*D*oubts are more cruel than the worst of truths.

MOLIÈRE

I don't think man comes to faith firsthand, except through despair, or to knowledge of God, except through doubt.

FRANCIS B. SAYRE

*S*erious doubt is confirmation of faith. It indicates the seriousness of the concern, its unconditional character.

PAUL TILLICH

Duty

A man's own natural duty, even if it seems imperfectly done, is better than work not naturally his own, even if this is well-performed.

BHAGAVAD-GITA

*U*nable to do your duty to the living, how can you do your duty to the dead? . . . Not yet understanding life, how can you understand death?

CONFUCIUS

*D*uty cannot exist without faith.

BENJAMIN DISRAELI

*W*hen Elijah was waiting with impatience for the divine Presence in the wilderness, he found that God was not clothed in the whirlwind or in the earthquake, but that He was in the still small voice of duty.

CHARLES E. GARMAN

*I*n duty the individual finds his liberation; liberation from dependence on mere natural impulse.

G. W. F. HEGEL

*T*he Church of God has to be the salt and light of the world. We are the hope of the hopeless, through the power of God. We must transfigure a situation of hate and suspicion, of broken-ness and separation, of fear and bitterness. We have no option. We are servant to the God who reigns and cares.

DESMOND TUTU

*D*uty is what one expects from others—it is not what one does oneself.

OSCAR WILDE

Ecumenism

*R*eligions now coexist and interact whether or not theologians or mullahs or bishops approve. Religious pluralism is an irreducible fact.

HARVEY COX

*W*e must openly accept all ideologies and systems as means of solving humanity's problems. One country, one nation, one ideology, one system is not sufficient.

FOURTEENTH DALAI LAMA

*L*et no one even for a moment entertain the fear that a reverent study of other religions is likely to weaken or shake one's faith in one's own. The Hindu system of philosophy regards all religions as containing the elements of truth in them and enjoins an attitude of respect and reverence towards them all.

MOHANDAS K. GANDHI

*I*t is unfair and unwise to try to understand one religion by the yardstick of another.

ARI GOLDMAN

I have to be a Hindu, a Buddhist, a Jain, a Parsee, a Sikh, a Muslim, and a Jew, as well as a Christian, if I am to know the Truth and to find the point of reconciliation in all religion.

BEDE GRIFFITHS

*B*y means of dialogue, we have come to see more clearly the many values, practices, and teachings that both our religious traditions [Christianity and Islam] embrace, for example, our beliefs in the one almighty and merciful God, creator of heaven and earth, and the importance that we give to prayer, almsgiving and fasting.

POPE JOHN PAUL II

*T*he pope—and we know this well—is without a doubt the most serious obstacle on the ecumenical road.

POPE PAUL VI

*N*othing is so foreign to the spirit of ecumenism as a false irenicism, in which the purity of Catholic doctrine suffers loss, and its assured genuine meaning is clouded.

SECOND VATICAN COUNCIL

I believe that if we really want human brotherhood to spread and increase until it makes life safe and sane, we must also be certain that there is no one true faith or path by which it may spread.

ADLAI E. STEVENSON

Education

*I*f students grow up ignorant of the role of religion, of religious freedom, and religious faith in American life, then surely we will have badly failed them.

WILLIAM BENNETT

*T*he parents have a right to say that no teacher paid by their money shall rob their children of faith in God and send them back to their homes skeptical, or infidels, or agnostics, or atheists.

WILLIAM JENNINGS BRYAN

*R*eal education consists in drawing the best out of yourself. What better book can there be than the book of humanity?

MOHANDAS K. GANDHI

*I*t is essential to the moral development of the child to start with some form of belief in the divine order, [a] framework he will at first take for Gospel truth until the spiritual content matures into symbolic interpretation.

ARTHUR KOESTLER

*T*here are those parents who deprive a spirit-hungry child of the sacramental fellowship of the Church, on the grounds that he is too young to understand. Well, we're all too young to understand.

JOHN E. LARGE

No church can sincerely subscribe to the theory that questions of faith do not enter into the education of children.

WALTER LIPPMANN

The only group secular education actually pleases is the atheistic.

FULTON SHEEN

Enlightenment

In this world, aspirants may find enlightenment by two different paths. For the contemplative is the path of knowledge; for the active is the path of selfless action.

BHAGAVAD-GITA

All thy rafters are broken, thy ridge-pole is sundered; thy mind, approaching Nirvana, has attained to extinction all desires.

DHAMMAPADA

In the full state of awareness, we accept everything and everybody unconditionally; we do not even conceptualize. Love flows, and our joy, our pleasure, our fun is enormous and incomplete.

DHIRAVAMSA

Keep quiet. Do your work in the world, but inwardly keep quiet. Then all will come to you.

NISARAGADA HA MAHARAJ

We stumble and fall constantly even when we are most enlightened. But when we are in true spiritual darkness, we do not even know that we have fallen.

THOMAS MERTON

A reencounter with original blessing is experienced as a leap to a new state of being that breaks the hold of false power upon our spirit. In this sense, it is psychologically experienced as something beyond our present state of existence. But . . . we know it to be the most natural thing in the world, since, when we encounter original blessing, we immediately recognize it as our true selves—something with which we are already gifted, not something we have to strive to achieve.

ROSEMARY RADFORD RUETHER

*G*oing back to the origin is called peace; it means reversion to destiny. Reversion to destiny is called eternity. He who knows eternity is called enlightened.

TAO TE CHING

*I*llumination means that the delusory distinction between the two shores of a worldly and transcendental existence no longer holds.

HEINRICH ZIMMER

Evil

The sad truth is that most evil is done by people who never make up their minds to be either good or evil.

HANNAH ARENDT

No evil could exist where no good exists.

ST. AUGUSTINE

Finding God in the history of the holocaust will help us come across Him in our private hells and holocausts. A religiosity which does not address itself to such tasks is slop!

LIONEL BLUE & JONATHAN MAGONET

It is right noble to fight with wickedness and wrong; the mistake is in supposing that spiritual evil can be overcome by physical means.

LYDIA M. CHILD

The belief in a supernatural source of evil is not necessary; men alone are quite capable of every wickedness.

JOSEPH CONRAD

The evil life is really the *thoughtless* life.

DHAMMAPADA

*N*on-cooperation with evil is as much a duty as is cooperation with good.

MOHANDAS K. GANDHI

*W*hat is evil but good tortured by its own hunger and thirst?

KAHLIL GIBRAN

*E*vil is here in the world, not because God wants it or uses it here, but because He knows not how at the moment to remove it; or knowing, has not the skill or power to achieve His end. Evil, therefore, is a fact not to be explained away, but to be accepted; and accepted not to be endured, but to be conquered. It is a challenge neither to our reason nor to our patience, but to our courage.

JOHN HAYNES HOLMES

*E*vil is the footstool of good, there is no absolute evil.

ISRAEL BEN ELIEZER

*N*o man is clever enough to know all the evil he does.

FRANÇOIS DE LA ROCHEFOUCAULD

*E*vil can no more be charged upon God than darkness can be charged upon the sun.

WILLIAM LAW

*I*t is a sin to believe evil of others, but it is seldom a mistake.

H. L. MENCKEN

*W*hen we deny the evil in ourselves, we dehumanize ourselves, and we deprive ourselves not only of our own destiny but of any possibility of dealing with the evil of others.

J. ROBERT OPPENHEIMER

*M*en never do evil so completely and cheerfully as when they do it from religious conviction.

BLAISE PASCAL

*U*nwittingly, evil serves as a beacon to warn others away from its own shoals.

M. SCOTT PECK

*E*vil is obvious only in retrospect.

GLORIA STEINEM

*W*e must love God through the evil that occurs, solely because everything that actually occurs is real and behind all reality stands God.

SIMONE WEIL

Faith & Reason

A person can do other things against his will; but belief is possible only in one who is willing.

ST. AUGUSTINE

*M*an's creed is that he believes in God, and therefore in mankind, but not that he believes in creed.

LEO BAECK

*T*rust God. If you surrender you must be able to abide by His will and not make grievance of what may not please you. Things may turn out different from what they are in appearance.

PAUL BRUNTON

*I*t is always easier to believe than to deny. Our minds are naturally affirmative.

JOHN BURROUGHS

A belief may be larger than a fact. A faith that is overdefined is the very faith most likely to prove inadequate to the great moments of life.

VANNEVAR BUSH

*I*t is not really a question of what a man is made to believe but of what he must believe; what he cannot help believing.

G. K. CHESTERTON

*M*y reason nourishes my faith and my faith my reason.

NORMAN COUSINS

I predict that in a postmodern world in which science, philosophy and theology have once again begun to communicate with each other, and in which politics and religion no longer inhabit different compartments of the same enterprise, the present unnatural separation between faith and intellect will also be transcended.

HARVEY COX

*M*an is a being born to believe, and if no church comes forward with all the title deeds of truth, he will find alters and idols in his own heart and his own imagination.

BENJAMIN DISRAELI

*W*ithout faith man becomes sterile, hopeless and afraid to the very core of his being.

ERICH FROMM

I do not feel obliged to believe that the same God who has endowed us with sense, reason and intellect, has intended us to forgo their use.

GALILEO

*A*ges of faith and of unbelief are always said to mark the course of history.

EDITH HAMILTON

*T*o rely on our faith would be idol-worship. We have only the right to rely on God.

ABRAHAM JOSHUA HESCHEL

*I*t is consciousness itself . . . which can suggest that there is God. For it is the hint that there can exist something very real that is more than the merely physical.

BARRY HOLTZ

*F*aith is not a momentary feeling, but a struggle against the discouragement that threatens us every time we meet with resistance.

BAKOLE WA ILUNGA

*F*aith branches off from the highroad before reason begins.

WILLIAM JAMES

*F*aith is required of thee, and a sincere life, not loftiness of intellect, nor deepness in the mysteries of God.

THOMAS À KEMPIS

*W*e want to believe in God. For all our celebration of our wondrous achievements, we don't really want to have ultimate responsibility for the world.

HAROLD KUSHNER

*R*eason is the greatest enemy that faith has: it never comes to the aid of spiritual things, but more frequently than not struggles against the divine Word, treating with contempt all that emanates from God.

MARTIN LUTHER

*T*he intellect is the link that joins us to God.

MOSES MAIMONIDES

*F*aith without skepticism is not faith. It is superstition.

SAMUEL MILLER

*I*f a man have a strong faith he can indulge in the luxury of skepticism.

FRIEDRICH NIETZSCHE

*I*t too often happens that the religiously disposed are in the same degree intellectually deficient.

JOHN HENRY NEWMAN

*B*elief is thought at rest.

CHARLES S. PIERCE

*F*ewer beliefs, more belief.

JAMES PIKE

*T*hose who believe and do not obscure their faith with wrong, they are those who shall have security and they are guided.

QUR'ĀN

*F*aith is an excitement and an enthusiasm: it is a condition of intellectual magnificence to which we must cling as to a treasure, and not squander on our way through life in the small coin of empty words, or in exact or priggish argument.

GEORGE SAND

*A*ll religions promise a reward . . . for excellences of the *will* or heart, but none for excellence of the head or understanding.

ARTHUR SCHOPENHAUER

*F*aith is the subtle chain which binds us to the infinite.

ELIZABETH OAKES SMITH

*F*aith and doubt both are needed—not as antagonists but
working side by side—to take us around the unknown curve.

LILLIAN SMITH

*T*o believe in something not yet proved and to underwrite it
with our lives; it is the only way we can leave the future open.
Man, surrounded by facts, permitting himself no surprise, no
intuitive flash, no great hypothesis, no risk, is in a locked cell.
Ignorance cannot seal the mind and imagination more securely.

LILLIAN SMITH

*R*eason, however sound, has little weight with ordinary
theologians.

BARUCH SPINOZA

*T*o keep the lamp burning, we have to keep putting oil in it.

MOTHER TERESA

*A*n act of faith is an act of a finite being who is grasped by and
turned to the infinite.

PAUL TILLICH

*F*aith is the sense of life, that sense by virtue of which man
does not destroy himself, but continues to live on. It is the force
whereby we live.

LEO TOLSTOY

*M*an discovers truth by reason only, not by faith.

LEO TOLSTOY

*I*f there is faith that can move mountains, it is faith in your own power.

MARIE EBNER VON ESCHENBACH

*B*elief without elements of terror and doubt is fairy tale, not faith.

DAVID WOLPE

Forgiveness

*M*an lives by getting and forgetting. God lives by giving and forgiving.

DIANA BASKIN

*F*orgiveness is not an occasional act; it is a permanent attitude.

MARTIN LUTHER KING, JR.

*W*e pardon in the degree that we love.

FRANÇOIS DE LA ROCHEFOUCAULD

*I*n the evening of life, we shall be judged on love, and not one of us is going to come off very well, and were it not for my absolute faith in the loving forgiveness of my Lord I could not call on him to come.

MADELEINE L'ENGLE

*E*veryone says forgiveness is a lovely idea, until they have something to forgive.

C. S. LEWIS

*S*in powerfully; God can forgive only a hearty sinner.

MARTIN LUTHER

*A*llah, Most High, says: He who approaches near to me one span, I will approach to him one cubit; and he who approaches near to me one cubit, I will approach near to him one fathom; and whoever approaches me walking, I will come to him running, and he who meets me with sins equivalent to the whole world, I will greet him with forgiveness equal to it.

MISHKAT-UL-MASABIH

God

*T*he way God has been thought of for thousands of years is no longer convincing; if anything is dead, it can only be the traditional *thought* of God.

HANNAH ARENDT

*G*od is not what you imagine or what you think you understand. If you understand you have failed.

ST. AUGUSTINE

*W*e can know what God is not, but we cannot know what He is.

ST. AUGUSTINE

*P*eople see God every day, they just don't recognize him.

PEARL BAILEY

*I*f the concept of God has any validity or any use, it can only be to make us larger, freer, and more loving. If God cannot do this, then it is time we got rid of Him.

JAMES BALDWIN

*E*ven those who are devoted to other gods, and sacrifice to them full of faith, are really worshipping me, though not in the prescribed fashion.

BHAGAVAD-GITA

*N*o one who seeks Brahman ever comes to an evil end.

BHAGAVAD-GITA

*H*e who would see the Divinity must see him in his Children.

WILLIAM BLAKE

*T*he Power which calls us to work in the world is itself 'apart', unworldly and holy. The nature of the 'apartness' and its identity is glimpsed in the burning bush, in Jacob's dream, or in the exchange between It and Moses on Mount Sinai.

LIONEL BLUE

*W*e are all strings in the concert of His job; the spirit from His mouth strikes the note and tune of our strings.

JAKOB BOEHME

*G*od made the angels to show him splendour.

ROBERT BOLT

*G*od is weak and powerless in the world, and that is precisely the way, the only way, in which he is with us and helps us. Only the suffering God can help.

DIETRICH BONHOEFFER

A God who would let us prove his existence would be an idol.

DIETRICH BONHOEFFER

*P*ut God underneath all your life, and your life must rest upon the everlasting arms.

PHILLIPS BROOKS

*T*he God of the "other religions" is always an idol.

EMIL BRUNNER

*T*he concept of God has become virtually synonymous with a goodness and a power that transcends us, an elusive, often static spirit beyond our reach, ontologically uninvolved with us.

KATIE G. CANNON

*G*od is to me that creative Force, behind and in the universe, who manifests Himself as energy, as life, as order, as beauty, as thought, as conscience, as love, and who is self-revealed supremely in the creative Person of Jesus of Nazareth.

HENRY SLOANE COFFIN

*F*or God is not a God of confusion but of peace.

1 CORINTHIANS 14:33

*W*hy indeed must "God" be a noun? Why not a verb—the most active and dynamic of all? . . . The anthropomorphic symbols for God may be intended to convey personality, but they fail to convey that God is Be-ing.

MARY DALY

*W*hen man substituted God for the Great Goddess he at the same time substituted authoritarian for humanistic values.

ELIZABETH GOULD DAVIS

*H*im I call a Brahmana from whom anger and hatred, pride and hypocrisy have dropped like a mustard seed from the point of a needle.

DHAMMAPADA

*P*erfectly to will what God wills, to want what he wants, is to have joy.

MEISTER ECKHART

*T*he less theorizing you do about God, the more receptive you are to his inpouring.

MEISTER ECKHART

*G*od can no more do without us than we can do without him.

MEISTER ECKHART

*T*he God that holds you over the pit of hell, much as one holds a spider, or some loathsome insect, over the fire, abhors you, and is dreadfully provoked; his wrath towards you burns like fire; he looks upon you as worthy of nothing else, but to be cast into the fire.

JONATHAN EDWARDS

*T*he deep emotional conviction of the presence of a superior reasoning power, which is revealed in the incomprehensible universe, forms my idea of God.

ALBERT EINSTEIN

*T*he soul of God is poured into the world through the thoughts of men.

RALPH WALDO EMERSON

*I*n the nineteenth century the problem was that God is dead; in the twentieth century the problem is that man is dead.

ERICH FROMM

God, to me, it seems, is a verb, not a noun, proper or improper.

R. BUCKMINSTER FULLER

I could prove God statistically. Take the human body alone— the chances that all the functions of an individual would just happen is a statistical monstrosity.

GEORGE GALLUP

God has no religion.

MOHANDAS K. GANDHI

I have no special revelations of God's will. My firm belief is that He reveals Himself daily to every human being, but we shut our ears to the 'still small voice.' We shut our eyes to the 'pillar of fire' in front of us.

MOHANDAS K. GANDHI

There is nothing in existence which is self-subsistent, save the Living and Self-sustaining God, in Whom subsists all other things.

ABU-HĀMID MUHAMMAD AL-GHAZĀLĪ

He does not prove the existence of God; existence *is* God.

J. W. VON GOETHE

Given this diversity of gods, each person is free to choose his or her own god or goddess. . . . If the Jews are the Chosen People, Hindus are the People who Choose God.

ARI GOLDMAN

*I*f ye do not recognize God, at least recognize His signs.

HUSAYN AL-HALLAJ

I am he whom I love, and he whom I love is I,
We are two spirits dwelling in one body,
If thou seest me, thou seest him,
And if thou seest him, thou seest us both.

HUSAYN AL-HALLAJ

I am the vessel. The draft is God's. And God is the thirsty one.

DAG HAMMARSKJÖLD

*G*od does not die on the day when we cease to believe in a
personal deity, but we die on the day when our lives cease to be
illumined by the steady radiance, renewed daily of a wonder,
the source of which is beyond all reason.

DAG HAMMARSKJÖLD

*T*he God of the Hebraic religion is either a living, active,
"feeling" God or He is nothing.

WILL HERBERG

*G*od is of no importance unless He is of supreme importance.

ABRAHAM JOSHUA HESCHEL

*T*o begin thinking about God, we suggested, is to understand
that there are things that we can never understand.

BARRY HOLTZ

*I*t is fear that first made the gods.

DAVID HUME

*G*od dwells in a secret and hidden way in all souls, in their very substance, for if he did not, they could not exist at all.

ST. JOHN OF THE CROSS

*C*alled or Not Called, God is Present.

STONE TABLET ABOVE
CARL JUNG'S DOOR

*I*t is not God who will save us, it is we who will save God—by battling, by creating, and by transmuting matter into spirit.

NIKOS KAZANTZAKIS

*T*he issue is not what God is like. The issue is what kind of people we become when we attach ourselves to God.

HAROLD KUSHNER

*A*ll gods were immortal.

STANISLAW LEM

*H*e, the universal God, is not born any time, nor does he ever die; nor will he ever cease to be. Unborn, everlasting, eternal.

MAHABHARATA

*T*he Supreme is subject to nothing. It is the Great Mother, and She holds you in the palm of her hand.

VIMALIA MCCLURE

*W*e speak of God as love, but are afraid to call God lover.

SALLIE MCFAGUE

*T*he metaphors of God as king, ruler, lord, master and governor, and the concepts that accompany them of god as absolute, complete, transcendent and omnipotent permit no sense of mutuality, shared responsibility, reciprocity, and love (except in the sense of gratitude).

SALLIE MCFAGUE

*A*s for myself, I am content with the conviction that God's eyes are ever upon me, and that his providence and justice will follow me into the future life as it has protected me in this.

MOSES MENDELSSOHN

*W*e find God in our own being which is the mirror of God.

THOMAS MERTON

*B*y withdrawing into intimate dialogue with God, man can attain the complete abandonment of his passions and evil habits, that is, he can free himself from the claims of his flesh and return to his source.

NAHMAN OF BRATSLAV

*I*f God be my friend I cannot be wretched.

OVID

*T*here is a God within us, and we glow when he stirs us.

OVID

*N*o matter how much we may like to pussyfoot around it, all of us who postulate a loving God eventually come to a single terrifying idea: God wants us to become Himself (or Herself or Itself). We are growing toward godhood. God is the goal of evolution.

M. SCOTT PECK

*I*mages of God as fountain, source, wellspring, or ground of life and being remind us that God loves and befriends us as one who brings forth all being and sustains it in existence.

JUDITH PLASKOW

*T*he earth, the sun and stars, and the universe itself; and the charming variety of the seasons, demonstrate the existence of Divinity.

PLATO

*N*o one who in early life has adopted this doctrine of the non-existence of gods has ever persisted to old age constant to that conviction.

PLATO

*A*llah! There is no God save Him, the living, the eternal! Neither slumber nor sleep overtaketh Him, unto Him belong whatsoever is in the earth. . . . He knoweth that which is behind them. . . . His throne includeth the heavens and the earth, and He is never weary of preserving them. He is the Sublime, the Tremendous.

QUR'ĀN

*W*e belong to God, and to Him we return.

QUR'ĀN

*G*od is, by definition, ultimate reality. And one cannot argue whether ultimate reality really exists. One can only ask what ultimate reality is like.

J. A. T. ROBINSON

*T*he existentialist finds it very troublesome that god does not exist, because with Him disappears all possibility of finding values in an intelligible world. . . . We are precisely on a plane where nothing exists but men.

JEAN PAUL SARTRE

*G*od is not finished. His highest divine attribute is His creativeness and that which is creative exists always in the beginning stage. God is eternally in Genesis.

ISAAC BASHEVIS SINGER

I hold that God is the immanent, and not the extraneous, cause of all things. I say, All is in God; all lives and moves in God.

BARUCH SPINOZA

*W*hatsoever is, is in God.

BARUCH SPINOZA

*T*he blessings of Wakan Tanka flowed over the Indian like rain showered from the sky. Wakan Tanka was not aloof, apart, and ever seeking to quell evil forces. He did not punish the animals and the birds, and likewise He did not punish man. . . . For there was never a question as to the supremacy of an evil power over and above the power of Good. There was but one ruling power, and that was *Good*.

CHIEF LUTHER STANDING BEAR

*G*iven the one concept, God, and the whole of reality bursts into lucidity; the rationality of the universe, its uniformity, the emergence of life, of consciousness, and conscience all become intelligible.

MILTON STEINBERG

*G*iven the one concept, God, and the whole of reality bursts into lucidity; the rationality of the universe, its uniformity, the emergence of life, of consciousness, and conscience all become intelligible.

MILTON STEINBERG

*T*here is no place to which we could flee from God which is outside God.

PAUL TILLICH

*B*rahman is supreme; he is self-luminous, he is beyond all thought. Subtler than the farthest, nearer than the nearest. He resides in the heart of every being.

UPANISHADS

*M*editate and you will realize that mind, matter, and Maya (the power which unites mind and matter) are but three aspects of Brahman, the one reality.

UPANISHADS

*H*e [Brahman] is the One God, hidden in all things, all-pervading, the Self within all beings, watching over all works, the Witness, the Perceiver, the only one free from qualities. . . . The wise who perceive Him within their self, to them belongs eternal happiness.

UPANISHADS

*J*ust as light is diffused from a fire which is confined to one spot, so is this whole universe the diffused energy of the supreme Brahman.

VISHNU, PURANAS

I have always believed in God, though I have my quarrels with Him. In the Jewish tradition, one may say no to God if it is on behalf of other people.

ELIE WIESEL

I believe that one can be a good Jew or Christian or Buddhist and be with God or against God, but not without God.

ELIE WIESEL

I sometimes think that God, in creating men, somewhat over-estimated his ability.

OSCAR WILDE

Goodness

Do not think that you are the person to effect any reform.
Leave these aims latent. Let God attend to them.

PAUL BRUNTON

True goodness springs from a man's own heart. All men are
born good.

CONFUCIUS

The great man is sparing in words but prodigal in deeds.

CONFUCIUS

To be proud of virtue is to poison yourself with the antidote.

BENJAMIN FRANKLIN

He who bears another, is borne by another.

ST. GREGORY THE GREAT

When good befalls a man he calls it Providence, when evil Fate.

KNUT HAMSUN

For as the body is clad in the cloth, and the flesh in the skin
and the bones in the flesh and the heart in the whole, so are
we, soul and body, clad in the goodness of God and enclosed.
Yea and more homely; for all these may wear and waste away,
but the Goodness of God is ever whole.

DAME JULIANA

*E*ternal life is not a life for the future. By charity we start eternity right here below.

HENRI DE LUBAC

*T*he tendency of man's nature to good is like the tendency of water to flow downwards.

MENCIUS

*T*here is a force that somehow pushes us to choose the more difficult path whereby we can transcend the mire and muck into which we are so often born.

M. SCOTT PECK

*T*he more merciful Acts thou dost, the more Mercy thou wilt receive.

WILLIAM PENN

*T*hose who have faith and do good works are the rightful owners of the Garden and will dwell in it.

QUR'ĀN

*W*e can do no great things; only small things with great love.

MOTHER TERESA

*G*oodness is the only investment that never fails.

HENRY DAVID THOREAU

*T*o the virtuous all is pure.

TRIPITAKA

Grace

*G*race is nothing else but a certain beginning of glory in us.

ST. THOMAS AQUINAS

*I*t is becoming impossible for those who mix at all with their fellow-men to believe that the grace of God is distributed denominationally.

WILLIAM RALPH INGE

*G*race is not a strange, magic substance which is subtly filtered into our souls to act as a kind of spiritual penicillin. Grace is unity, oneness within ourselves, oneness with God.

THOMAS MERTON

*A*mazing grace! How sweet the sound,
That saved a wretch like me;
I once was lost, but now I'm found;
Was blind, but now I see.

JOHN NEWTON

*A*ll men who live with any degree of serenity live by some assurance of grace.

REINHOLD NIEBUHR

The religious, who, of course, ascribe the origins of grace to God, believing it to be literally God's love, have through the ages had the same difficulty locating God. There are within theology two lengthy and opposing traditions in this regard: one, the doctrine of Emanance, which holds that grace emanates down from an eternal God to men; the other the doctrine of Immanence, which holds that grace immanates out from the God within the center of man's being.

M. SCOTT PECK

The grace of God is in my mind shaped like a key, that comes from time to time and unlocks the heavy doors.

DONALD SWAN

Guilt

We are all exceptional cases. . . . Each man insists on being innocent, even if it means accusing the whole human race, and heaven.

ALBERT CAMUS

I am suspicious of guilt in myself and in other people; it is usually a way of not thinking, or of announcing one's own fine sensibilities the better to be rid of them fast.

LILLIAN HELLMAN

This is his first punishment, that by the verdict of his own heart no guilty man is acquitted.

JUVENAL

We have no choice but to be guilty.
God is unthinkable if we are innocent.

ARCHIBALD MACLEISH

Not wishing to be other than they are, the blameless ones, in their self-love, cannot conceive the real alternative: another self, cleansed of guilt and freed from folly, capable of renewal.

LEWIS MUMFORD

*B*elief in Some One's right to punish you is the fate of all children in Judaic–Christian culture. But nowhere else, perhaps, have the rich seedbeds of Western homes found such a growing climate for guilt as produced in the South by the combination of warm moist evangelism and racial segregation.

LILLIAN SMITH

Heresy

*R*eligions are kept alive by heresies, which are really sudden explosions of faith. Dead religions do not produce them.

G. BRENAN

*H*eresy is only another word for freedom of thought.

GRAHAM GREENE

*A*void heretics like wild beasts; for they are mad dogs, biting secretly.

ST. IGNATIUS OF ANTIOCH

*C*hrist himself and his apostolic followers, by the standards existing in their day, were "heretical."

RUFUS M. JONES

*T*he heresy of one age becomes the orthodoxy of the next.

HELEN KELLER

*I*n all ages the tendency of the heretic has been to single out one aspect of Christian life or doctrine, and treat it as if it were the whole.

RONALD A. KNOX

There is never a devout saint or believer in universal love who is not a "heretic" to some other believer, whether Christian or Buddhist.

LIN YÜ-T'ANG

Wherever there is a creed there is a heretic round the corner or in his grave.

ALFRED NORTH WHITEHEAD

Hinduism

*S*o long as a Hindu conforms to the customs and practices of his society, he may believe what he likes.

P. N. BASU

*A*lthough Hindu thought has been unambiguous in its recognition that spiritual values overshadow all earthly considerations, it has never been half-hearted in acknowledging the importance of worldly obligations.

SIVAPRASAD BHATTACHARYYA

*H*induism as a religion is centered not so much in the belief in God, as in faith in the reality of spirit and the spiritual order of the world.

SATIS BANKIM CHATTERJEE

*T*he complexity of Hinduism is so great, the forms which it assumes are so protean, that it defies precise definition.

L. S. S. O'MALLEY

*H*induism teaches that all creatures, as long as they are creatures, are involved in this time process which is called *samsara,* the state of each creature in any particular life depending upon the good or evil it has done in its preceding lives.

D. S. SARMA

*H*indus sometimes pride themselves, with some truth, that their religion is free from dogmatic assumptions, and that, this being so, their record in the matter of religious persecution is relatively clear.

R. C. ZAEHNER

Holy Days

[The Sabbath] was not, at first, a day for cultic acts or long worship services. It was a time set aside for affirming what is.

HARVEY COX

[The Native American] sees no need for setting apart one day in seven as a holy day, because to him all days are God's days.

CHARLES ALEXANDER EASTMAN

The Sabbath is the choicest fruit and flower of the week, the Queen whose coming changes the humblest home into a palace.

JUDAH HALEVI

The Sabbaths are our great cathedrals.

ABRAHAM JOSHUA HESCHEL

The first thing that is expressed in the Jewish passover is the certainty of freedom. With the Exodus a new age was struck for humanity: redemption from misery. If the Exodus had not taken place, marked as it was by the twofold sign of the overriding will of God and the free and conscious assent of men, the historical destiny of humanity would have followed another course.

ANDRE NEHER

*E*aster means—hope prevails over despair. Jesus reigns as Lord of Lords and King of Kings. Oppression and injustice and suffering can't be the end of the human story. Freedom and justice, peace and reconciliation, are his will for all of us, black and white, in this land and throughout the world. Easter says to us that despite everything to the contrary, his will for us will prevail, love will prevail over hate, justice over injustice and oppression, peace over exploitation and bitterness.

DESMOND TUTU

Hope

*W*hat oxygen is to the lungs, such is hope to the meaning of life.

EMIL BRUNNER

*I*f you do not hope, you will not find what is beyond your hopes.

ST. CLEMENT OF ALEXANDRIA

I do not think that man will disappear, not even in an atomic holocaust. I always believe in the creativity of the human spirit.

MIRCEA ELIADE

*W*e must accept finite disappointment, but we must never lose infinite hope.

MARTIN LUTHER KING, JR.

*E*verything that is done in the world is done by hope.

MARTIN LUTHER

*N*othing that is worth doing can be achieved in a lifetime; therefore we must be saved by hope.

REINHOLD NIEBUHR

*H*ope is the source of all happiness. . . . None is to be considered a man who does not hope in God.

PHILO

*H*ope deferred makes the heart sick,
but a desire fulfilled is a tree of life.

PROVERBS 13:12

*T*he miserable have no other medicine,
But only hope.

WILLIAM SHAKESPEARE

*T*rue to the heart of Jewish religious belief, above both faith and reason, hope reigns supreme.

MILTON STEINBERG

*W*ithin us we have a hope which always walks in front of our present narrow experience; it is the undying faith in the infinite in us.

RABINDRANATH TAGORE

*C*athedrals are an unassailable witness to human passion. Using what demented calculation could an animal build such places? I think we know. An animal with a gorgeous genius for hope.

LIONEL TIGER

*H*ope, like faith, is nothing if it is not courageous; it is nothing if it is not ridiculous.

THORNTON WILDER

Humanity

God did not call you to be canary-birds in a little cage, and to hop up and down on three sticks, within a space no larger than the size of the cage. God calls you to be eagles, and to fly sun to sun, over continents.

HENRY WARD BEECHER

Underneath expensive wrappings, I found loneliness, selfishness, spiritual decay, and egomania out of sync with human caring and a sense of mutuality.

MALCOLM BOYD

The word of him who wishes to speak with god without speaking with men goes astray.

MARTIN BUBER

When you see your brother, you see God.

ST. CLEMENT OF ALEXANDRIA

Always trust your fellow man. And always cut the cards.

ROBERT FULGHUM

God created humankind so that humankind might cultivate the earthly and thereby create the heavenly.

HILDEGARD OF BINGEN

*M*an is a fallen god who remembers the heavens.

ALPHONSE DE LAMARTINE

*O*h God! that man should be a thing for immortal souls to sieve through!

HERMAN MELVILLE

*A*ll people are a single nation.

QUR'ĀN

A new society is not built by those who are only capable of machinating violence and destruction, but by those who work in generous dedication, some of them in silence or suffering, in favor of their neighbors.

POPE JOHN PAUL II

*M*odern man is master of his fate. What he suffers he suffers because he is stupid or wicked, not because it is nature's decree.

BERTRAND RUSSELL

*T*he significance of our lives and our fragile realm derives from our own wisdom and courage. We are the custodians of life's meaning. We would prefer it to be otherwise, of course, but there is no compelling evidence for a cosmic Parent who will care for us and save us from ourselves.

CARL SAGAN

*I*n looking backward, we must renew our faith in God. In looking forward, we must renew our faith in men.

ROBERT SANCHEZ

The human spirit is a glass through which we can peer more deeply into reality than by purely rational instruments alone.

EDMUND SINNOTT

Wonders are many, and none is more wonderful than man.

SOPHOCLES

Man is the great experiment of God.

GEORGE M. TREVELYAN

Man is a Religious Animal. He is the only Religious Animal. He is the only animal that has the True Religion—several of them. He is the only animal that loves his neighbor as himself and cuts his throat if his theology isn't straight.

MARK TWAIN

The essential contradiction in the human condition is that man is subject to force, and craves for justice. He is subject to necessity, and craves for the good.

SIMONE WEIL

What is man but his passion?

ROBERT PENN WARREN

Man is not an end but a beginning. We are at the beginning of the second week. We are children of the eighth day.

THORNTON WILDER

Human Relationships

*T*he union of man and wife is from God, so divorce is from the devil.

ST. AUGUSTINE

*I*f a man divorces his first wife, even the altar sheds tears.

BABYLONIAN TALMUD

*T*o my mind, divorce is a deplorable breach of contract, and I say without humor that children should be allowed to sue.

ARI GOLDMAN

*C*hristian marriage is essential and indissoluble. You must resist the pressures of the times and worldly currents, sometimes eroding from within, that lead to the dissolution of Christian law and values.

POPE JOHN PAUL II

*W*e are all made for marriage, as our bodies show and as the Scriptures state.

MARTIN LUTHER

*W*hoever does the will of God is my brother, and sister, and mother.

MARK 3:35

*T*rain up a child in the way he should go,
and when he is old he will not depart from it.

PROVERBS 22:6

*Y*e may divorce your wives twice; keep them honorably, or put
them away with kindness.

QUR'ĀN

A marriage which really works is one which works for others.
Marriage has both a private face and a public importance.

ROBERT RUNCIE

*T*oo many married people expect their partner to give that
which only God can give, namely, an eternal ecstasy.

FULTON SHEEN

Humility

*N*othing is more scandalous than a man who is proud of his humility.

MARCUS AURELIUS

I am but the least among the least, small is my understanding and timid my heart.

BAUDONIVIA

*M*an how contemptible thou dost appear!
What art thou in this scene?—Alas no more
Than a small atom to the sandy shore,
A drop of water to a boundless sea,
A single moment to eternity.

ANN ELIZA BLEECKER

*N*o man is an island, entire of itself; every man is a piece of the Continent, a part of the main . . . any man's death diminishes me, because I am involved in Mankind and therefore never send to know for whom the bell tolls; it tolls for thee.

JOHN DONNE

*T*he feelings of my smallness and my nothingness have always kept me good company.

POPE JOHN XXIII

*D*o nothing from selfishness or conceit, but in humility count others better than yourselves.

PHILIPPIANS 2:3

*A*fter all the great religions have been preached and expounded, or have been revealed by brilliant scholars, or have been written in books and embellished in fine language with fine covers, man—all man—is still confronted with the Great Mystery.

CHIEF LUTHER STANDING BEAR

*M*y heart and I lie small upon the earth like a grain of throbbing sand.

ZITAKALA-SA

Immortality

O mighty among men, he is fit to attain immortality who is serene and not afflicted by these sensations, but is the same in pleasure and pain.

BHAGHAVAD-GITA

*H*e who, at the time of death, thinking of Me alone, goes forth, leaving the body, he attains unto my Being.

BHAGAVAD-GITA

*I*f I err in my belief that the souls of men are immortal, I err gladly, and I do not wish to lose so delightful an error.

CICERO

*I*f something comes to life in others because of you, then you have made an approach to immortality.

NORMAN COUSINS

*T*he body dies but the spirit is not entombed.

DHAMMAPADA

*T*he blazing evidence of immortality is our dissatisfaction with any other solution.

RALPH WALDO EMERSON

God is the producer of immortality; and who ever had doubts of immortality is written down as an atheist without trial.

WILLIAM JAMES

If I find in myself a desire which no experience in this world can satisfy, the most probable explanation is that I was made for another world.

C. S. LEWIS

I believe with perfect faith that there will be a revival of the dead at the time when it shall please the Creator.

MOSES MAIMONIDES

The life to come will be better for thee than the life thou livest, for the bounty of the Lord shall come to thee.

QUR'ĀN

It is not possible that we should remember that we existed before our body, for our body can bear no trace of such existence, neither can eternity be defined in terms of time or have any relation to time. But notwithstanding, we feel and know that we are eternal.

BARUCH SPINOZA

When Judaism speaks of immortality . . . its primary meaning is that man contains something independent of the flesh and surviving it; his consciousness and moral capacity; his essential personality, a soul.

MILTON STEINBERG

Going back to the origin is called peace; it means reversion to destiny. Reversion to destiny is called eternity. He who knows eternity is called enlightened.

TAO TE CHING

*T*he less a man believes in the soul . . . the more he will
exaggerate the worth of this poor transitory life.

MIGUEL DE UNAMUNO Y JUGO

*O*ur birth is but a sleep and a forgetting;
The soul that rises with us, our life's star,
Hath had elsewhere its setting,
And cometh from afar.

WILLIAM WORDSWORTH

Islam

*U*ntil college and minaret have crumbled
This holy work of ours will not be done.
Until faith becomes rejection, and rejection becomes belief
There will be no true Muslim.

ABA SAIID IBN ABI KHAYR

*L*ike other faiths, Islam struggles with the question of human
suffering and why some prayers are answered and some are not.
One teaching says that man is like the nightingale. God keeps
man in cages because he loves the music of his prayers. If he is
slow to answer, it is only because He loves the song and does
not want it to end.

ARI GOLDMAN

*I*slam is a completion of the heritage of Moses and Abraham
and Jesus, a continuation of the heritage of all the prophets.

AHMAD ZAK HAMMAD

*I*slam is practical, and not only a contemplative religion. It
teaches certain social rules of communal behavior and lays down
a relationship between the government and those it governs.

HASSAN II

Jesus

*W*e have lost a Prophet. We miss, even to our own day, the golden page of the sayings of Jesus; that, however, was the price we paid in order that the Jewish genius might give the world a redeemer who brought it under the authority of God.

SHOLEM ASCH

*I*f he [Jesus] is not in the ghetto, if he is not where human beings are living at the brink of existence, but is, rather, in the easy life of the suburbs, then the gospel is a lie.

JAMES CONE

*C*hrist must be rediscovered perpetually.

EDITH HAMILTON

*H*e is all the world's hero, the desire of nations. But besides he is the hero of single souls.

GERARD MANLEY HOPKINS

*M*an is soon changed and lightly falleth away, but Christ abideth for ever and standeth strongly with his lover unto the end.

THOMAS À KEMPIS

*M*any, as has been well said, ran after Christ, not for the miracles, but for the loaves.

JOHN LUBBOCK

*T*ake Jesus out of the perfumed cloisters of pious sentiment, and let him walk the streets of the city.

PETER MARSHALL

*T*he truth is, it is not Jesus as historically known, but Jesus as spiritually arisen within men, that is significant for our time, and can help it.

ALBERT SCHWEITZER

*T*he Galilean has been too great for our small hearts.

H. G. WELLS

*I*n every decade we instruct Christ as to what he was and is, instead of allowing ourselves to be instructed by him.

AMOS WILDER

Jewish–Christian Relationship

*J*ews have God's promise and if we Christians have it, too, then it is only as those chosen with them, as guests in their house, that we are new wood grafted onto their tree.

KARL BARTH

*H*e who does not himself remember that God led him out of Egypt . . . is no longer a true Jew.

MARTIN BUBER

*J*esus was a Jew. There is nothing that the ordinary Christian so dislikes to remember as this awkward historical fact.

JOHN HAYNES HOLMES

*Y*ou are our dearly beloved brothers, and in a certain way, it could be said that you are our elder brothers.

POPE JOHN PAUL II

*A*nti-Semitism is a form of Christian hypocrisy. The Christian whitewashes himself by attributing his views to the Jew.

BERNARD LAZARE

I was born Jewish and so I remain, even if that's unacceptable for many. For me, the vocation of Israel is bringing light to the goyim. That's my hope and I believe that Christianity is the means for achieving it.

JEAN MARIE CARDINAL LUSTIGER

*I*t is not possible for Christians to take part in anti-Semitism. We are Semites spiritually.

POPE PIUS XI

Judaism

As long as the world lasts, all who want to make progress for righteousness will come to Israel for inspiration.

MATTHEW ARNOLD

As long as Judaism continues, nobody will be able to say that the soul of man has allowed itself to be subjugated.

LEO BAECK

If humility is Christianity, you, Jews, are true Christians!

WILLIAM BLAKE

[The Jew] was not created to be a religious automaton, or a human prayer wheel. He has to assimilate God's command into himself, and this means argument at the deepest level of his being. Holy argument is the greatest path to God in Jewish experience, and dialectic is as effective for a Jew as a rosary is for a Catholic, in approaching the Almighty.

LIONEL BLUE

The Jews gave to the world its three greatest religions, reverence for law, and the highest conceptions of morality.

LOUIS BRANDEIS

I don't believe there are epiphanies in Judaism. Since it is a religion that insists on concrete deeds, not on blinding revelations of Divine Power, a newcomer like me who decides to become part of it has to do so slowly, one mitzvah at a time, in order to transform himself without losing himself.

PAUL COWAN

*F*or decades I had felt a silent inexplicable raging grief over the feeling that I was an orphan in history, a dazed member of a lost tribe. I realized I was no longer an orphan in time, but a wandering Jew who had come home.

PAUL COWAN

*F*or the Catholic [communion] is total submission. Open your mouth and the wafer is placed there. . . . It is entirely different from the Jewish approach; the Jew must work for his redemption, whether at the kiddush table, in the study hall, or in the marketplace.

ARI GOLDMAN

*J*udaism is a *religion of time* aiming at the *sanctification of time.*

ABRAHAM JOSHUA HESCHEL

*I*srael was made to be a "holy people." This is the essence of its dignity and the essence of its merit.

ABRAHAM JOSHUA HESCHEL

*E*ntering the world of Jewish texts about God, we enter a world of constantly shifting images. In that palace of metaphors each of us can find a place.

BARRY HOLTZ

*W*e . . . advocate the elimination from our own liturgy of all references to the doctrine of Israel as the Chosen People.

MORDECAI M. KAPLAN

The preservation of the Jews is really one of the most signal and illustrious acts of divine Providence.

THOMAS NEWTON

In traditional society, Jews may have been outsiders, but they had an important defense against indifference or hatred; their own communal self-understanding radically contradicted the world outside. In the modern world, Jews have more deeply internalized society's expectations and values, becoming divided from the Jew within the self.

JUDITH PLASKOW

This power of being a minority, a persecuted minority, and staying with one's culture for 2,000 years, denies all sociological theories.

ISAAC BASHEVIS SINGER

There is a mystery about the Jews . . . and within this mystery lies the reason for the folk pride of the house of Abraham. This pride exists despite the disabilities that come from many centuries of ostracism.

HERMAN WOUK

Justice

*L*et justice roll down like waters,
and righteousness like an everflowing stream.

AMOS 5:24

*U*nder the Guru's instruction regard all men as equal, since
God's light is contained in the heart of each.

ARJAN

*I*f faith does anything, as shown by the prophets and Jesus, it
leads us into the injustice and suffering in the world.

DANIEL BERRIGAN

*R*ecompense injury with justice and recompense kindness with
kindness.

CONFUCIUS

*T*ruth is the summit of being; justice is the application of it to
affairs.

RALPH WALDO EMERSON

A person who lacks the verdancy of justice is dry, totally
without tender goodness, totally without illuminating virtue.

HILDEGARD OF BINGEN

*J*ustice is truth in action.

JOSEPH JOUBERT

*J*ustice is so subtle a thing, to interpret it one has only need of a heart.

JOSE GARCIA OLIVER

A God all mercy is a God unjust.

EDWARD YOUNG

Knowledge

*T*he raft of knowledge ferries the worst sinner to safety.

BHAGAVAD-GITA

*F*or we can only know that we know nothing, and a little knowledge is a dangerous thing.

CHUANG-TZU

I believe that the expansion of knowledge makes for an expansion of faith, and the widening of the horizons of mind for a widening of belief.

NORMAN COUSINS

*T*he tree of knowledge is the tree of death.

BENJAMIN DISRAELI

*F*or in much wisdom is much grief: and he that increases knowledge increases sorrow.

ECCLESIASTES 1:18

*S*piritual ignorance is often so complete that people do not realize they are ignorant.

T. D. MUNDA

Life

Life, the permission to know death.

DJUNA BARNES

The messiness of experience. That may be what we mean by life.

DANIEL BOORSTIN

[I]t is . . . our task to create foretastes of . . . what life is *meant* to be, which include art and music and poetry and shared laughter and picnics and politics, and moral outrage and special privileges for children only and wonder and humor and endless love, to counterbalance the other immobilizing realities of tyrants, starving children, death camps, and just plain greed.

ROBERT MCAFEE BROWN

Life is a pure flame, and we live by an invisible sun within us.

THOMAS BROWNE

Nothing about the Universe is more complex, more resistant to the penetrating powers of systematic thought, more diverse in its manifestations, more elusive in its antecedents, more electrifying in its capacities, than human life itself.

NORMAN COUSINS

*R*everence for life is more than solicitude or sensitivity for life. It is a sense of the whole, a capacity for inspired response, a respect for the intricate universe of individual life. It is the supreme awareness of awareness itself.

NORMAN COUSINS

*D*reading death, I've discovered I can still affirm life.

PAUL COWAN

*L*ife is an incurable disease.

ABRAHAM COWLEY

*W*hat is life but the flower or the fruit which falls, when ripe, but yet which ever fears the untimely frost?

DHAMMAPADA

*T*hough our natural life were no life, but rather a continual dying, yet we have two lives besides that, an eternal life reserved for heaven, but yet a heavenly life too, a spiritual life, even in this world.

JOHN DONNE

*U*ntil you know that life is interesting—and find it so—you haven't found your soul.

GEOFFREY FISHER

*T*he finest hours are not those spent among large groups of people, but in converstaion with just a few, in reading great books, in listening to great music, wandering in a forest of qiant sequoia, peering into a microscope, unraveling nature's secrets in a laboratory.

JOEL HILDEBRAND

*O*ur heart glows, and secret unrest gnaws at the root of our being. . . . Dealing with the unconscious has become a question of life for us.

CARL JUNG

A day spent without the sight or sound of beauty, the contemplation of mystery, or the search for truth and perfection, is a poverty-stricken day; and a succession of such days is fatal to human life.

LEWIS MUMFORD

*E*verything in life is most fundamentally a gift. And you receive it best and you live it best by holding it with very open hands.

LEO O'DONOVAN

*L*iving is strife and torment, disappointment and love and sacrifice, golden sunsets and black storms. I take a simple view of living. It is keep your eyes open and get on with it.

LAURENCE OLIVIER

*L*ife is perhaps best regarded as a bad dream between two awakenings.

EUGENE O'NEILL

*O*ur lives are merely strange dark interludes in the electrical display of God the Father.

EUGENE O'NEILL

*I*f we have to play the game of life, we cannot do so with the conviction that the play is a show and all the prizes in it mere blanks.

SAVREPALLI RADHAKRISHNAN

*E*verything we are and have on this pilgrimage from womb to tomb belongs to God; we are but stewards of whatever we have been given charge of—life, death, body, mind, spirit, family, friends, community, and whatever of the wealth of the Planet Earth's crust is entrusted to us.

JAMES A. SANDERS

*T*here's no place a man can escape to now. Like art, life itself is a risk and a hazard in its very nature. It's always fragmentary, never complete. Its validity is in the adventure.

ISAAC BASHEVIS SINGER

*L*ife is God's novel. Let him write it.

ISAAC BASHEVIS SINGER

*O*ne wears his mind out in study, and yet has more mind with which to study. One gives away his heart in love, and yet has more heart to give away. One perishes out of pity for a suffering world, and is the stronger therefore. So, too, it is possible at one and the same time to hold life and let it go.

MILTON STEINBERG

*L*ife is to live in such a way as not to be afraid to die.

ST. TERESA OF AVILA

*L*et us so live that when we come to die even the undertaker will be sorry.

MARK TWAIN

*L*ife is misery, and miraculous beauty.

JANWILLEM VAN DE WETERING

Loneliness

*W*hat loneliness is more lonely that distrust?

GEORGE ELIOT

*W*hen you have shut your doors and darkened your room, remember never to say that you are alone, for you are not alone, but God is within, and your genius is within.

EPICTETUS

*L*oneliness is dangerous. It's bad for you to be alone, to be lonely, because if aloneness does not lead to God, it leads to the devil. It leads to the self.

JOYCE CAROL OATES

*M*an's loneliness is but his fear of life.

EUGENE O'NEILL

*L*oneliness is bred of a mind that has grown earthbound. For the spirit has its homeland, which is the realm of the meaning of things.

ANTOINE DE SAINT-EXUPÉRY

*L*oneliness and the feeling of being unwanted is the most terrible poverty.

MOTHER TERESA

*T*he soul hardly ever realizes it, but whether he is a believer or not, his loneliness is really a homesickness for God.

HUBERT VAN ZELLER

Love

*I*t is only the souls that do not love that go empty in this world.

ROBERT HUGH BENSON

I know no one in any time who has succeeded in loving every man he met.

MARTIN BUBER

*L*ove is patient and kind; love is not jealous or boastful; it is not arrogant or rude. Love does not insist on its own way; it is not irritable or resentful; it does not rejoice at wrong, but rejoices in the right. Love bears all things, believes all things, hopes all things, endures all things.

1 CORINTHIANS 13:4–7

*L*ove is the central theme in the biblical view of life. The opposite of love, however, is not hatred. It is possessiveness, the deep-set human drive to control and own the other.

HARVEY COX

*W*e have all known the long loneliness and we have learned that the only solution is love.

DOROTHY DAY

*I*f a man lives a hundred years, and engages the whole of his time and attention in religious offerings to the gods, sacrificing elephants and horses and other things all this is not equal to one act of pure love in saving life.

DHAMMAPADA

*F*or hatred does not cease by hatred at any time: Hatred ceases by love, this is an old rule.

DHAMMAPADA

*L*ove is just love, or love *is;* the concept of "divine" or "human" doesn't make any difference to love. For love does not discriminate; it only unites and unifies everything.

DHIRAVAMSA

*L*ove can do all but raise the Dead.

EMILY DICKINSON

*L*ove is the noblest frailty of the mind.

JOHN DRYDEN

I never give thanks to God for loving me because he cannot help it; whether he would or not it is his nature to.

MEISTER EKHART

*N*o soul is desolate as long as there is a human being for whom it can feel trust and reverence.

GEORGE ELIOT

*T*he moment we exercise our affections, the earth is metamorphosed; there is no winter, and no night; all tragedies, all ennuis vanish—all furies even.

RALPH WALDO EMERSON

*L*ove is the abridgement of all theology.

ST. FRANCIS DE SALES

*L*ove is the strongest force the world possesses, and yet it is the humblest imaginable.

MOHANDAS K. GANDHI

*L*ove for God is the furthest reach of all stations, the sun of the highest degrees, and there is no station after that of love, except its fruit and its consequences.

ABU-HĀMID MUHAMMAD AL-GHAZĀLĪ

*O*ur present economic, social and international arrangements are based, in large measure, upon organized lovelessness.

ALDOUS HUXLEY

*"T*hou shalt love thy neighbor as thyself." Why? Because every human being has a root in the Unity, and to reject the minutest particle of the Unity is to reject it all.

ISREAL BEN ELIEZER

*L*ove is the only force capable of transforming an enemy into a friend.

MARTIN LUTHER KING, JR.

*H*e who defends with love will be secure; Heaven will save him, and protect him with love.

LAO-TZU

*W*e have much to be judged on when he comes, slums and battlefields and insane asylums, but these are the symptoms of our illness and the result of our failures in love.

MADELEINE L'ENGLE

*T*he love of our neighbor is the only door out of the dungeon of
self.

GEORGE MACDONALD

*L*ove is will, the will to share your happiness with all. Being
happy—making happy—this is the rhythm of love.

NASARAGADA HA MAHARAJ

*M*an's love of god is identical with his knowledge of him.

MOSES MAIMONIDES

*I*n a battle of wills, loving kindness is the only weapon that
conquers.

VIMALIA MCCLURE

*I*f the relationship between lovers is arguably the deepest
human relationship, then it should be a central metaphor for
modeling some aspects of the God—world relationship.

SALLIE MCFAGUE

*L*ove begins only when the ego renounces its claim to absolute
autonomy and ceases to live in a little kingdom of desires in
which it is its own end and reason for existing.

THOMAS MERTON

*L*ove is a union of wills. The perfect love of God is a perfect
union of wills with God: that means the inability to will
anything that God does not will.

THOMAS MERTON

*I*n a spiritual life there is no such thing as an indifference to
love or hate. That is why tepidity (which seems to be
indifferent) is so detestable. It is hate disguised as love.

THOMAS MERTON

The love of God in its essence is really the illumination of the heart of joy because of its nearness to the beloved.

HARITH IBN-ASAD AL-MUHASIBI

Love is not the product of any particular religion. It is the rightful province of each and every human heart.

T. D. MUNDA

Love is sure to be something less than human if it is not something more.

COVENTRY PATMORE

What love does in transfiguring life . . . religion does in transfiguring love.

COVENTRY PATMORE

The idea that we are loved for what is most valuable in us, that God sees our worth even when we cannot, is far more conducive to human empowerment and accountability than the idea that we are loved despite our worthlessness.

JUDITH PLASKOW

Is it too much to ask why God seems to continue to love us, why God has not walked off and abandoned us as a bad experiment?

JAMES A. SANDERS

Love is a mutual self-giving which ends in self-recovery.

FULTON SHEEN

Someday, after mastering the winds, the waves, the tides and gravity, we shall harness for God the energies of love, and then, for a second time in the history of the world, man will have discovered fire.

PIERRE TEILHARD DE CHARDIN

I am a little pencil in the hand of a writing God who is sending a love letter to the world.

MOTHER TERESA

*L*ove has a hem to her garment that reaches to the very dust. It sweeps the stains from the streets and lanes, and because it can, it must.

MOTHER TERESA

*T*he first duty of love is to listen.

PAUL TILLICH

*M*ystic love is a total dedication of the will; the deep-seated desire and tendency of the soul towards its Source.

EVELYN UNDERHILL

*T*o love is not a state; it is a direction.

SIMONE WEIL

*I*f we love only through what is good, then it is not God we are loving but something earthly to which we give that name.

SIMONE WEIL

*N*obody is worthy to be loved. The fact that God loves man shows us that in the divine order of ideal things it is written that eternal love is to be given to what is eternally unworthy.

OSCAR WILDE

*T*here is a land of the living and a land of the dead and the bridge is love, the only survival, the only meaning.

THORNTON WILDER

Materialism & Greed

A fool bolts pleasure, then complains of moral indigestion.

MINNA ANTRIM

*Y*ou will derive your supreme satisfaction not from your ability to amass things or to achieve superficial power but from your ability to identify yourselves with others and to share fully in their needs and hopes. In short, for fulfillment, we look to identification rather than acquisition.

NORMAN COUSINS

*H*ow easy it is for a poor man to depend on God! What else has he to depend on? And how hard it is for a rich man to depend on God! All his possessions call out to him: "Depend on us!"

MOSHE LEIB (ATTRIBUTED)

*N*o one can serve two masters; for either he will hate the one and love the other, or he will be devoted to the one and despise the other. You cannot serve God and mammon.

MATTHEW 6:24

*G*od is ashamed when the prosperous boast of his special favor.

RABINDRANATH TAGORE

Morality & Ethics

*H*illel said: What is hateful to you, do not do to your neighbor: that is the whole Torah; the rest is commentary; go, study.

BABYLONIAN TALMUD

*I*t is in God that morality has its foundation and guarantee.

LEO BAECK

*T*he world has achieved brilliance without wisdom, power without conscience. Ours is a world of nuclear giants and ethical infants.

OMAR BRADLEY

A morality without God is as weak as a traffic law when the policeman is on foot.

WILL DURANT

*L*earn to call white white and black black, evil evil and good good. Learn to call sin sin and do not call it liberation and progress, even if all out of fashion.

POPE JOHN PAUL II

*I*t is God's will, not merely that we should *be* happy, but that we should make ourselves happy. This is true morality.

IMMANUEL KANT

I am always suspicious of public morality. Public morality is like public patriotism—a mask for scoundrels.

WILLIAM MCGILL

A man is truly ethical only when he obeys the compulsion to help all life which he is able to assist, and shrinks from injuring anything that lives.

ALBERT SCHWEITZER

*M*orality isn't the light; it is only the polish on the candlestick.

BILLY SUNDAY

*T*o say that there is no basis for personal and social ethics apart from one or another of the organized religions is untrue to observed fact and immensely derogatory to a God worth respecting.

NORMAN THOMAS

Music

When I think of God, my heart is so filled with joy that the notes fly off as from a spindle.

JOSEPH HAYDN

The body is truly the garment of the soul, which has a living voice; for that reason it is fitting that the body, simultaneously with the soul, repeatedly sings praises to God through the voice.

HILDEGARD OF BINGEN

Music is Love in search of a word.

SIDNEY LANIER

It is in music, perhaps, that the soul most nearly attains the great end for which, when inspired by the Poetic Sentiment, it struggles—the creation of supernal Beauty.

EDGAR ALLAN POE

The church knew what the psalmist knew: Music praises God. Music is well or better able to praise him than the building of the church and all its decoration: it is the Church's greatest ornament.

IGOR STRAVINSKY

*T*he God of Music dwelleth out of doors.

EDITH THOMAS

*M*usic hath caught a higher pace than any virtue that I know. It is the arch-reformer; it hastens the sun to its setting; it invites him to his rising; it is the sweetest reproach, a measured satire.

HENRY DAVID THOREAU

Nature

God made the beauties of nature like a child playing in the
sand.

APOLLONIUS OF TYANA (ATTRIBUTED)

Nature is name for an effect, whose cause is God.

WILLIAM COWPER

Nature is a rag merchant who works up every shred and ort
and end into new creations.

RALPH WALDO EMERSON

Great teachers take no credit for their students' growth, yet
they will go to any length to teach them what they need to
know. Nature requires no praise, yet it provides for the needs of
the earth's inhabitants.

VIMALIA MCCLURE

The heavens are telling the glory of God;
and the firmament proclaims his handiwork.

PSALM 19:1

Defy the commandments of the natural law, and the race will
perish in a few generations; co-operate with them, and the race
will flourish for ages to come.

DOROTHY SAYERS

*N*ature is neutral. Man has wrested from nature the power to make the world a desert or to make the deserts bloom. There is no evil in the atom; only in men's souls.

ADLAI E. STEVENSON

*N*ature is the school-mistress, the soul the pupil; and whatever one has taught or the other learned has come from God—the Teacher of the teacher.

TERTULLIAN

*N*ature is an appalling spectacle! Crushing! So in the midst of all this crushing, what shelters are there but bed and church? And maybe a book now and then.

JOHN UPDIKE

*T*he only gospel one ought to read is the great book of Nature, written by the hand of God and sealed with his seal. The only religion that ought to be professed is the religion of worshipping God and being a good man.

VOLTAIRE

Old Age

[*A*]s the outer shell wears thin, sometimes an inner light shows up more clearly—as in Rembrandt's portraits of old people.

LIONEL BLUE & JONATHAN MAGONET

*T*he years of old age . . . are indeed formative years, rich in possibilities to unlearn the follies of a lifetime, to see through inbred self-deceptions, to deepen understanding and compassion, to widen the horizon of honesty, to refine the sense of fairness.

ABRAHAM JOSHUA HESCHEL

*T*he real dread of men is not the devil, but old age.

EDGAR WATSON HOWE

*O*ld age, to the unlearned, is winter; to the learned, it is harvest time.

YIDDISH PROVERB

*D*ying while young is a boon in old age.

YIDDISH PROVERB

Pleasure & Joy

*B*lessed are You, Lord our God, King of the Universe, Whose love is manifest in laughter.

LIONEL BLUE

*T*he Devil invites men to the water of death . . . and blinding them with the pleasures and conditions of the world, he catches them with the hook of pleasure.

CATHERINE OF SIENA

*L*aughter does not seem to be a sin, but it leads to sin.

JOHN CHRYSOSTOM

*T*hat thou mayest have pleasure in everything, seek pleasure in nothing.

ST. JOHN OF THE CROSS

*O*ur loving God wills that we eat, drink, and be merry.

MARTIN LUTHER

*L*earning to laugh at ourselves, we did not lack other things to laugh about. How should we, if the Christian life is indeed the knowledge of him who is the author of laughter as well as tears?

MICHAEL RAMSEY

Poverty

*N*o one should commend poverty but the poor.

ST. BERNARD OF CLAIRVAUX

*P*overty is very good in poems, but it is very bad in a house. It is very good in maxims and in sermons, but it is very bad in practical life.

HENRY WARD BEECHER

*T*he rich man may never get into heaven, but the pauper is already serving his time in hell.

ALEXANDER CHASE

*P*overty is the open-mouthed, relentless hell which yawns beneath civilized society. And it is hell enough.

HENRY GEORGE

*T*he poor don't know that their function in life is to exercise our generosity.

JEAN-PAUL SARTE

*I*t is not the man who has little, but he who desires more, that is poor.

SENECA

*F*irst bread, and then religion. We stuff them too much with religion, when the poor fellows have been starving. No dogmas will satisfy the cravings of hunger.

SWAMI VIVEKANANDA

Prayer & Meditation

*P*rayer is the pillow of religion.

ARAB PROVERB

*P*rayer is the service of the heart.

BABYLONIAN TALMUD

*T*he wish to pray is a prayer in itself.

GEORGES BERNANOS

*H*e who labors as he prays lifts his heart to God with his hands.

ST. BERNARD OF CLAIRVAUX

*B*e careful about blessings. Your prayers may not change the world, but they may change you, and this is not really what you intended.

LIONEL BLUE

*B*y praying thus, with deep humility and faith, thou wilt merge into the heart of . . . the Divine Father–Mother, in a halo of rainbow light, and attain Buddhahood.

BOOK OF THE DEAD (TIBETAN)

I believe that God prays in us and through us, whether we are praying or not (and whether we believe in God or not). So, any prayer on my part is a conscious response to what God is already doing in my life.

MALCOLM BOYD

*"W*hy don't you write some prayers for stockbrokers?"
"I thought most prayers in the Episcopal Church *had* been written for stockbrokers."

MALCOLM BOYD

*P*rayer for many is like a foreign land. When we go there, we go as tourists. Like most tourists, we feel uncomfortable and out of place. Like most tourists, we therefore move on before too long and go somewhere else.

ROBERT MCAFEE BROWN

*H*e who offends against heaven has none to whom he can pray.

CONFUCIUS

*F*or me meditation is not a mystical experience. It is almost the opposite. It forces me to pare back daydreams, cut through rosy expectations and look carefully, often even painfully, at what is actually there in front of me and inside me.

HARVEY COX

*A*bsence of daily prayer is the disease of daily conversation.

DHAMMAPADA

*B*e not forgetful of prayer. Every time you pray, if your prayer is sincere, there will be new feeling and new meaning in it, which will give you fresh courage, and you will understand that prayer is an education.

FYODOR DOSTOYEVSKY

*P*rayer should be the key of the morning and the lock of the night.

OWEN FELLTHAM

*T*o pray is to desire; but it is to desire what God would have us desire.

FRANÇOIS FÉNELON

*O*n our knees we are the most powerful force on earth.

BILLY GRAHAM

*I*n crisis, in moments of despair, a word of prayer is like a strap we take hold of when tottering in a rushing street car which seems to be turning over.

ABRAHAM JOSHUA HESCHEL

*P*rayer is our humble answer to the inconceivable surprise of living.

ABRAHAM JOSHUA HESCHEL

*P*rayer, we like to hope, is a moment of true speaking. At that instant we become the words we say. There is no deception, no ego to defend, no manufactured self.

BARRY HOLTZ

*O*ne can only pray for what is possible. Facts cannot be changed. History cannot be reversed. Petitionary prayer must make sense in a world of reason.

BARRY HOLTZ

*P*ray, for all men need the aid of the gods.

HOMER

*M*editation is not the means to an end. It is both the means and the end.

JIDDU KRISHNAMURTI

*P*rayer does not use up artificial energy, doesn't burn up any fossil fuel, doesn't pollute.

MARGARET MEAD

*T*hrough prayer we can carry in our heart all human pain and sorrow, all conflicts and agonies, all torture and war, all hunger, loneliness, and misery, not because of some great psychological or emotional capacity, but because God's heart has become one with ours.

HENRI NOUWEN

*L*ike an opiate, sin drugs a conscience to drowsiness and stupor. Prayer stabs it wide awake.

JOHN A. O'BRIEN

*P*rayer is the drowning and unconsciousness of the soul.

JALĀL AD-DĪN AR-RŪMĪ

*Y*ank some of the groans out of your prayers, and shove in some shouts.

BILLY SUNDAY

*I*f you talk to God, you are praying; if God talks to you, you have schizophrenia.

THOMAS SZASZ

To pray is to descend with the mind into the heart, and there to stand before the face of the Lord, ever-present, all-seeing, within you.

THEOPHAN THE RECLUSE

Prejudice

I recognize no rights but *human* rights—I know nothing of men's rights and women's rights; for in Christ Jesus there in neither male nor female. It is my solemn conviction that, until this principal of equality is recognized and embodied in practice, the church can do nothing effectual for the permanent reformation of the world.

ANGELINA GRIMKÉ

A great many people think they are thinking when they are rearranging their prejudices.

WILLIAM JAMES

*W*e must use time creatively, in the knowledge that the time is always ripe to do right. Now is the time to make real the promise of democracy and transform our pending national elegy into a creative psalm of brotherhood. Now is the time to lift our national policy from the quicksand of racial injustice to the solid rock of human dignity.

MARTIN LUTHER KING, JR.

*I*t is disgraceful that people are being barred from neighborhoods and clubs on a basis that would have barred Jesus himself.

JAMES PIKE

*A*t the central moment of Jewish history [Exodus 19:15], women are invisible. Whether they too stood there trembling in fear and expectation, what they heard when the men heard these words of Moses, we do not know.

JUDITH PLASKOW

*T*he apartheid practiced toward women by the Church's rulers violates justice, much as political apartheid does.

UTA RANKE-HEINEMANN

*E*very type of discrimination whether social or cultural, whether based on sex, race, color, social condition, language or religion, is to be overcome and eradicated as contrary to God's intent.

SECOND VATICAN COUNCIL

*T*o see God as male is idolatry. It is like the worship of images in man's own shape.

BARBARA THIERING

*W*hy does suffering single out black people so conspicuously, suffering not at the hand of pagans or other unbelievers, but at the hands of white fellow Christians who claim allegiance to the same Lord and Master?

DESMOND TUTU

*Y*ou can't hold a man down without staying down with him.

BOOKER T. WASHINGTON

*R*acism is stupid, just as it is ugly. Its aim it to destroy, to pervert, to distort innocence in human beings and their quest for human equality.

ELIE WIESEL

Qur'ān

*C*an they not consider the *Qur'ān*? Were it from any other than God, they would have found in it many contradictions.

QUR'ĀN

*N*o translation, however faithful to the meaning, has ever been successful. . . . The Arabic of the *Qur'ān* is by turns striking, soaring, vivid, terrible, tender and breathtaking.

JOHN ALDEN WILLIAMS

Redemption

*H*e became what we are that he might make us what he is.

ST. ATHANASIUS

*F*or no one is redeemed except through unmerited mercy, and no one is condemned except through merited judgement.

ST. AUGUSTINE

*N*o one can be redeemed by another. No God and no saint is able to shield a man from the consequence of his evil doings. Every one of us must become his own redeemer.

SUBHADNA BHIKSHU

*N*ever be misled by the thought that after failing and sinning there can be no forgiveness. Look critically at your own shortcomings, but be sure that, with the Lord, there is always abundance of redemption.

BRAKKENSTEIN COMMUNITY
OF BLESSED SACRAMENT FATHERS

*I*f you are cut down in a movement that is designed to save the soul of a nation, then no other death could be redemptive.

MARTIN LUTHER KING, JR.

*T*his is the month, and this the happy morn,
Wherein the Son of Heaven's eternal King,
Of wedded maid, and virgin mother born,
Our great redemption from above did bring,
For so the holy sages once did sing,
That he our deadly forfeit should release
And with His Father work us a perpetual peace.

JOHN MILTON

*R*edemption: Not an instantaneous deed, but a life-long adventure.

MAX C. OTTO

*W*hat does being redeemed in Christ mean if you are a Jew about to be gassed?

ROBERT RUNCIE

I believe in Michaelangelo, Velasquez, and Rembrandt; in the might of design, the mystery of color, the redemption of all things by Beauty everlasting, and the message of Art that has made these hands blessed.

GEORGE BERNARD SHAW

A present deliverance from sin, a restoration of the soul to its primitive health, its original purity, a recovery of the divine nature.

JOHN WESLEY

Reincarnation

*T*he spiritual perfection which opens before man is the crown of long, patient, millennial outflowing of the Spirit in life and nature. This belief in a gradual spiritual progress and evolution is the secret of the almost universal Indian acceptance of the truth of reincarnation.

SRI AUROBINDO

I have run through a course of many births looking for the maker of this dwelling and not finding him; birth again and again is painful.

DHAMMAPADA

*A*ll things return eternally, and ourselves with them: We have already existed in times without number, and all things with us.

FRIEDRICH NIETZSCHE

*H*aving obtained a human birth, if you miss your chance, You'll fall back into the whirlpool of Existence, to receive blow after blow.

SAKI

*T*he dead shall rise, life shall return to the bodies, and they shall breathe again. . . . The whole physical world shall become free from old age and death, from corruption and decay, forever and ever.

. *ZEND-AVESTA*

· *173* ·

Religion

*Y*ou catch religion, like you catch measles, from people—as much from what they are as from what they say.

LIONEL BLUE

A secular culture falsifies the world, for it ignores the highest level of significance in the drama of existence.

BEN ZION BOKSER

*I*t may be that religion is dead, and if it is, we had better know it and set ourselves to try to discover other sources of moral strength before it is too late.

PEARL S. BUCK

*T*he miracles of the church seem to me to rest not so much upon faces or voices of healing power coming suddenly near to us from afar off, but upon our perceptions being made finer, so that for a moment our eyes can see and our ears can hear what is there about us always.

WILLA CATHER

*M*en will wrangle for religion; fight for it; die for it; anything but live for it.

C. C. COLTON

*T*here are moments in the lives of all men when you feel yourself completely belonging to something larger, nobler, more permanent than yourself. This experience is the religious experience.

JOHN DEWEY

*T*he soul of a civilization is its religion, and it dies with its faith.

WILL & ARIEL DURANT

I would no more quarrel with a man because of his religion than I would because of his art.

MARY BAKER EDDY

*I*t was the experience of mystery—even if mixed with fear— that engendered religion.

ALBERT EINSTEIN

*R*eligion is . . . the emotion of reverence which the presence of the universal mind ever excites in the individual.

RALPH WALDO EMERSON

*L*ike a river damned by its own ice, religion is held back by its congealed formulations.

HARRY EMERSON FOSDICK

*W*here there is fear there is no religion.

MOHANDAS K. GANDHI

*R*eligion, like every other form of absolutism, should be above justification.

HEINRICH HEINE

*R*eligion is a disease, but it is a noble disease.

HERACLITUS

*R*eligion has become an impersonal affair, an institutional loyalty. It survives on the level of activities rather than in the stillness of commitment.

ABRAHAM JOSHUA HESCHEL

A religious man is a person who holds God and man in one thought at one time, at all times, who suffers harm done to others, whose greatest passion is compassion, whose greatest strength is love and defiance of despair.

ABRAHAM JOSHUA HESCHEL

A consciously accepted system of make-believe.

ALDOUS HUXLEY

*T*o become a popular religion, it is only necessary for a superstition to enslave a philosophy.

WILLIAM RALPH INGE

*I*n the name of religion, one tortures, persecutes, builds pyres. . . . There is nothing in common between the means and the end, the means go far beyond the end . . . ideologies and religion . . . are the alibis of the means.

EUGÈNE IONESCO

*R*eligion is a monumental chapter in the history of human egotism.

WILLIAM JAMES

The great religions have as yet no common vocabulary or theological way of speaking, and this makes it necessary to take a stand within the framework of one religious tradition.

WILLIAM JOHNSTON

Religion is a perception of the Divine existence, issuing in duty.

MORRIS JOSEPH

Whatever else it is—let us be clear about that from the outset—religion is something we belong to, not something which belongs to us; something that has got hold of us, not something we have got hold of.

RONALD A. KNOX

Religion is the frozen thought of men out of which they build temples.

JIDDU KRISHNAMURTI

True religion teaches us not how to *win* friends but how to *be* a friend, to be concerned with alleviating the loneliness of others, learning to hear their cry instead of wondering why no one hears ours.

HAROLD KUSHNER

A religion without the element of mystery would not be a religion at all.

EDWIN LEWIS

Religion is a temper, not a pursuit.

HARRIET MARTINEAU

*I*t is doubtless true that religion has been the world's psychiatrist throughout the centuries.

KARL MENNINGER

*R*eligion is a candle inside a multi-colored lantern. Everyone looks through a particular color, but the candle is always there.

MOHAMMED NAGUIB

*N*atural religion . . . finds a God who is majestic, but not majestic enough to threaten human self-esteem.

REINHOLD NIEBUHR

*R*eligion in its true sense emphasizes the insight into our experiences and the consciousness that insists upon learning something from them.

CAROL OCHS

*M*en hate and despise religion, and fear it may be true.

BLAISE PASCAL

*T*he modern hatred of religion is hatred of the truth, hatred of all sublimity, hatred of the laughter of the gods. It is puerile human vanity trying to justify itself by a lie.

GEORGE SANTAYANA

*R*eligion is the metaphysics of the masses.

ARTHUR SCHOPENHAUER

*T*o us the ashes of our ancestors are sacred and their resting place is hallowed ground. You wander far from the graves of your ancestors and seemingly without regret. Your religion was written upon tables of stone by the iron finger of your God so that you could not forget. . . . Our religion is the traditions of our ancestors—the dreams of old men, given them in solemn hours of night by the Great Spirit; . . . and it is written in the hearts of our people.

CHIEF SEATTLE

*R*eligion is the supreme art of humanity.

ABBA HILLEL SILVER

*W*hen the Lakota heart was filled with high emotion, he danced. When he felt the benediction of the warming rays of the sun, he danced. When his blood ran hot with success of the hunt or chase, he danced. When his heart was filled with pity for the orphan, the lonely father, or bereaved mother, he danced. All the joys and exaltations of life, all his gratefulness and thankfulness, all his acknowledgments of the mysterious power that guided life, and all his aspirations for a better life, culminated in one great dance—the Sun Dance.

CHIEF LUTHER STANDING BEAR

*T*he Bible and Church have been the greatest stumbling blocks in the way of woman's emancipation.

ELIZABETH CADY STANTON

*R*eligion is never devoid of emotion, any more than love is. It is not a defect of religion, but rather its glory, that it speaks always the language of feeling.

D. E. TRUEBLOOD

*T*he first sign of your becoming religious is that you are becoming cheerful.

SWAMI VIVEKANANDA

*R*eligion insofar as it is a source of consolation is a hindrance to true faith.

SIMONE WEIL

*R*eligion is what the individual does with his own solitariness.

ALFRED NORTH WHITEHEAD

*S*ome religious people abolish hatred because they're religious. Others are fanatical, and they invoke hatred because they are religious.

ELIE WIESEL

Repentance & Atonement

*T*he sinning is the best part of repentance.

ARAB PROVERB

*C*hrist saved one thief at the last gasp, to show that there may be late repentance.

JOHN DONNE

*R*epentance was perhaps best defined by a small girl: It's to be sorry enough to quit.

C. H. KILMER

*A*tonement, rather than growth, is the aim of the religious confessional, whereas psychotherapy does not require that you feel sorry for your sins so long as you outgrow them!

JOSHUA LOTH LIEBMAN

*L*et not a repentant sinner imagine that he is remote from the estate of the righteous because of the sins and misdeeds that he has done. This is not true, for he is beloved and precious to God as if he had never sinned.

MOSES MAIMONIDES

*T*he confessional in the humblest Catholic Church in the world is a more efficacious agency for a complete catharsis than the office of any psychoanalyst.

JOHN A. O'BRIEN

*T*o utter forth our sin, merits the remission of sin.

ORIGEN

A sincere repenter of faults is like him who hath committed none.

QUR'ĀN

*T*hey who after they have done a base deed or committed a wrong against themselves, remember God, and implore forgiveness of their sins—and not persevere in what they have wittingly done amiss; as for these! Pardon from the Lord shall be their recompense.

QUR'ĀN

*R*epentance is not self-regarding, but God-regarding. It is not self-loathing, but God-loving.

FULTON SHEEN

*R*epentance is not only a realization of failure, not only a burst of contrition for having failed the good, not only a readiness to admit this failure freely . . . but also a determination not to fail the good again.

DOUGLAS V. STEERE

*T*o confess a fault freely is the next thing to being innocent of it.

PUBLILUS SYRUS

*W*hile it abases the man, it raises him; while it covers him with squalor, it renders him more clean, while it accuses, it excuses; while it condemns, it absolves.

TERTULLIAN

Saints & Prophets

Saintliness is also a temptation.

JEAN ANOUILH

A saint is a dead sinner, revised and edited.

AMBROSE BIERCE

The prophet is appointed to oppose the king, and even more: history.

MARTIN BUBER

In his holy flirtation with the world, God occasionally drops a handkerchief. These handkerchiefs are called saints.

FREDERICK BUECHNER

There is no liberation without prophets.

BAKOLE WA ILUNGA

A minor saint is capable of loving minor sinners. A great saint loves great sinners.

ISRAEL BEN ELIEZER

What makes saintliness . . . , as distinguished from ordinary goodness, is a certain quality of magnanimity and greatness of soul that brings life within the circle of the heroic.

HARRIET BEECHER STOWE

Salvation

There is no inconsistency between creation and salvation; for the one Father has employed the same agent for both works, effecting the salvation of the world through the same Word who made it in the beginning.

ST. ATHANASIUS

Salvation is not putting a man into Heaven, but putting Heaven into man.

MALTBIE D. BABCOCK

Whenever there is a withering of the Law and an uprising of lawlessness on all sides, *then* I manifest Myself. For the salvation of the righteous and the destruction of such as do evil, I come to birth age after age.

KRISHNA TO ARJUNA, BHAGAVAD-GITA

Salvation is not actualized only in the last moment of one's life, or only in eternity. It is anticipated. The human being must enter upon a whole salvation process, a process that begins here on earth and ends in eternity.

LEONARDO BOFF

There is one thing we most of us forget. Christ taught it. The Church teaches it . . . though you wouldn't think so to hear a great many of us today. No one in good faith can ever be lost.

A. J. CRONIN

The process of salvation must come from within.

DHAMMAPADA

As long as there is the rhythm of day and night, winter and summer, man will continue to dream, to believe in being saved. The idea of being renewed is part of the cycle—you feel it every spring.

MIRCEA ELIADE

No man has the right to abandon the care of his salvation to another.

THOMAS JEFFERSON

The essence of religion is the human quest for salvation.

MORDECAI M. KAPLAN

For the gate is narrow and the way is hard, that leads to life, and those who find it are few.

MATTHEW 7:14

There is no such thing as a single scheme of salvation. Salvation is not the monopoly of any church. All paths lead to the hilltop of one and the same God-consciousness. The different religions are suited to the different aspirants in their various stages of progress.

SWAMI NIKHILANANDA

To save one's soul is not an instantaneous deed, but a life-long adventure.

MAX C. OTTO

*T*his is the way Jesus saves us: by revealing the nature of God and by creating within us the desire for fellowship with Him; by exhibiting life as it ought to be and may be and thus inspiring us to nobler conduct.

KIRBY PAGE

*W*hat is most contrary to salvation is not sin but habit.

CHARLES-PIERRE PEGUY

I must keep up my running argument with God, but in doing so I must also never let myself forget one thing: It is man to whom He gave the means to achieve ultimate salvation and God's own redemption—the key to the orchard of knowledge.

ELIE WIESEL

*G*od must be prodded by the prayers of human beings to effect his own salvation! If God cannot seek salvation alone, surely human beings cannot.

DAVID WOLPE

Science & Religion

*W*hat do I care if the heavens are a circumambient sphere and not a sort of dishcover?

ST. AUGUSTINE

*S*cience is daily more and more personified and anthropomorphized into a god.

SAMUEL BUTLER

*T*he cosmic religious experience is the strongest and noblest driving force behind scientific research.

ALBERT EINSTEIN

*R*eligion is about values; science about the factual state of the world. They are different enterprises, and there's no more reason for them to be at loggerheads than music and ditchdigging.

STEPHEN JAY GOULD

*I*t is no longer possible to maintain that science and religion must operate in thought-tight compartments or concern separate sections of life; they are both relevant to the whole of human existence.

JULIAN HUXLEY

*S*cience investigates; religion interprets. Science gives man knowledge which is power; religion gives man wisdom which is control. Science deals mainly with facts; religion deals mainly with values. The two are not rivals. They are complementary.

MARTIN LUTHER KING, JR.

*B*oth the man of science and the man of action live always at the edge of mystery, surrounded by it.

J. ROBERT OPPENHEIMER

*I*n some sort of crude sense in which no vulgarity, no humor, no overstatement can quite extinguish, the physicists have known sin: and this is a knowledge which they cannot lose.

J. ROBERT OPPENHEIMER

*F*or the most part both the religious and the scientific remain in self-imposed narrow frames of reference, each still largely blinded by its own particular type of tunnel vision.

M. SCOTT PECK

*N*othing stands in our way—and our instinctive intellectual striving for a unified world picture demands it—from identifying with each other the two everywhere active and yet mysterious forces: the world order of natural science and the God of religion.

MAX PLANCK

*S*cience has made the world a neighborhood, but it will take love to make it a sisterhood, a brotherhood, a community of peace with justice.

ELIZABETH M. SCOTT

*F*ormerly, when religion was strong and science weak, men mistook magic for medicine; now, when science is strong and religion weak, men mistake medicine for magic.

THOMAS SZASZ

*N*either in its impetus nor in its achievements can science go to its limits without becoming tinged with mysticism and faith.

PIERRE TEILHARD DE CHARDIN

*S*cience is getting down to the nitty-gritty and God is showing through.

JOHN UPDIKE

*W*hat we certainly have is our instinctive intellectual curiosity about the universe from the quasars down to the quarks, our delight and wonder at existence itself, and an occasional surge of sheer blind gratitude for being here.

JOHN UPDIKE

Self

*W*hen one finds one's Self, one has found God; and finding God one has found one's Self.

ANANDAMAYI MA

*P*eace is not to be found in the continual seeking for gratification of the separated self. . . . It is found in renouncing the separated self, in resting on the Self that is One, the Self that is manifesting at every stage of evolution.

ANNIE BESANT

*W*e talk of attaining the Self, of reaching God with time. There is nothing to attain. We are already Self-Existent.

PAUL BRUNTON

*T*he need is not to amputate the ego but to transcend it.

NORMAN COUSINS

*G*od asks only one thing of you: that you dethrone the creaturely self and let Him be God in you.

MEISTER ECKHART

*T*o atone is to be at one with God, to sink self into the not-self, to achieve a mystic unity with the source of being, wiping out all error and finding peace in self-submergence.

ISAAC GOLDBERG

*I*t is precisely in this pure poverty when one is no longer a "self" that one recovers one's true identity in God: This true identity is the "birth of Christ in us."

THOMAS MERTON

*T*his divine likeness in us which is the core of our being and is "in God" even more than it is "in us," is the focus of God's inexhaustible creative delight.

THOMAS MERTON

*I*n order to approach the Absolute, mystics must withdraw from everything, even themselves.

E. RECEJAC

*H*ell is the ego, sated with its own satisfied wishes, having to consume itself forever with no hope of release.

FULTON SHEEN

*T*he ego, being a flimsy construction and being bound up in time and space, will have to fall apart. The ego, in fact, continuously falls apart and has to be reinforced by vanity, greed, jealousy and evil.

JANWILLEM VAN DE WETERING

Silence & Solitude

Silence is the mother of truth.

BENJAMIN DISRAELI

Silence is the cornerstone of character.

CHARLES ALEXANDER EASTMAN

There is nothing in all creation so like God as stillness.

MEISTER ECKHART

Solitude is bearable only with God.

ANDRÉ GIDE

The men who have had the most to give to their fellow men are those who have enriched their minds and hearts in solitude. It is a poor education that does not fit a man to be alone with himself.

JOEL HILDEBRAND

Silences are the only scrap of Christianity we still have left.

SØREN KIERKEGAARD

Solitude is the furnace of transformation.

HENRI NOUWEN

A man may seem to be silent, but if his heart is condemning others he is babbling ceaselessly. But there may be another who talks from morning till night and yet he is truly silent.

ABBA POEMEN

*B*e still, and know that I am God.

PSALM 46:11

*S*olitude vivifies; isolation kills.

JOSEPH ROUX

*T*he world would be happier if men had the same capacity to be silent that they have to speak.

BARUCH SPINOZA

*W*e need no wings to go in search of Him, but have only to find a place where we can be alone—and look upon Him present within us.

ST. TERESA OF AVILA

*W*e must always take sides. Neutrality helps the oppressor, never the victim. Silence encourages the tormentor, never the tormented.

ELIE WIESEL

Sin

A private sin is not so prejudicial in this world as a public indecency.

MIGUEL DE CERVANTES

*A*s long as the sin bears no fruit, the fool, he thinks it honey; but when the sin ripens, then, indeed, he goes down in sorrow.

DHAMMAPADA

*T*hat which we call sin in others is experiment for us.

RALPH WALDO EMERSON

*I*n the liberation approach sin is not considered as an individual, private, or merely interior reality—asserted just enough to necessitate a "spiritual" redemption which does not challenge the order in which we live. Sin is regarded as a social, historical fact, the absence of brotherhood and love in relationships among men, the breach of friendship with God and with other men.

GUSTAVO GUTIERREZ

*T*he greatest of all sins is the philosophizing of sin out of existence.

HAROLD GARDINER

*S*in has many tools, but a lie is the handle that fits them all.

OLIVER WENDELL HOLMES

*O*ur specific status is in our very creatureliness, not in our specific deeds.

C. S. LEWIS

I think we all sin by needlessly disobeying the apostolic injunction to "rejoice" as much as by anything else.

C. S. LEWIS

*N*o poor fellow chained in sin, dead, and bound for hell can ever hear anything more comforting and encouraging than this precious and lovely message about Christ.

MARTIN LUTHER

*S*in is rebellion against God; it is a traitor's act who aims at the overthrow and death of his sovereign. . . . Sin is the moral enemy of the All-holy, so that He and it cannot be together.

JOHN HENRY NEWMAN

*M*an is a sinner not because he is finite but because he refuses to admit that he is.

REINHOLD NIEBUHR

*O*nly a fool could deny the fact of sin, though we may choose to call it by another name.

GERALD VANN

Soul

The life whereby we are joined into the body is called the soul.

ST. AUGUSTINE

The soul which is not moved,
The soul that with a strong and constant calm
Takes sorrow and takes joy indifferently,
Lives in the life undying!

BHAGAVAD-GITA

The white man has lost his soul. But he is so small-minded that he has confused his soul with God.

VINE DELORIA, JR.

The purity of the flesh is set down to the credit of virtue, but true virtue is of the soul, not of the body.

HÉLOISE

Our soul is *made* to be God's dwelling place; and the dwelling place of the soul is God, which is *unmade*.

JULIAN OF NORWICH

The soul is the mirror of an indestructible universe.

G. W. LEIBNIZ

*A*nd I say let a man be of good cheer about his soul. When the soul has been arrayed in her own proper jewels—temperance and justice and courage and nobility and truth—she is ready to go on her journey when the time comes.

SOCRATES

*W*e can think of the soul not as an entity but as a principle.

D. T. SUZUKI

*T*he soul is naturally Christian.

TERTULLIAN

*T*he human being is born with two desires. . . . And they are called the two dynamics of the soul. The will to live and the will to worship.

IRINA TWEEDIE

*T*he danger is not lest the soul should doubt whether there is any bread, but lest, by a lie, it should persuade itself that it is not hungry.

SIMONE WEIL

Spirituality

There are four things in which every man must interest himself. Who am I? Wherefore have I come from? Whither am I going? How long shall I be here? All spiritual inquiry begins with these questions and attempts to find out the answers.

DIANA BASKIN

To see a world in a grain of sand,
And a heaven in a wild flower,
Hold infinity in the palm of your hand
And eternity in an hour.

WILLIAM BLAKE

One of the disconcerting facts about the spiritual life is that God takes you at your word.

DOROTHY DAY

Spirituality for me is the sum total of all the acts of my day, waking with a prayer, eating kosher, sharing with my friends, even, in my mother's constellation, taking out the garbage. Judaism makes everything holy, ties me back to history and connects me with the spirit of God.

ARI GOLDMAN

*T*he kind of spiritual communion our forebears knew is less
accessible to us—because the world is so noisy and full of
distractions, because we are so dazzled by our power and
success, because religion in the late twentieth century is often
badly packaged or presented by people we cannot trust or
admire.

HAROLD KUSHNER

*L*et each one remember that he will make progress in all
spiritual things only insofar as he rids himself of self-love, self-
will and self-interest.

SAINT IGNATIUS OF LOYOLA

*S*pirituality lies in regarding existence merely as a vehicle for
contemplation, and contemplation merely as a vehicle for joy.

GEORGE SANTAYANA

*T*here is no dichotomy between spirit and flesh, no split
between Godhead and the world. . . . Spiritual union is found
in life, within nature, passion, sensuality—through being fully
human, fully one's self.

STARHAWK

*T*he spiritual life . . . means the ever more perfect and willing
association of the invisible Divine Spirit for all purposes; for the
glory of God, for the growth and culture of the praying soul.

EVELYN UNDERHILL

Strength

O, do not pray for easy life. Pray to be stronger men. Do not pray for tasks equal to your powers. Pray for powers equal to your tasks.

PHILLIPS BROOKS

*T*he first question to be answered by any individual or any social group, facing a hazardous situation, is whether the crisis is to be met as a challenge to strength or as an occasion for despair.

HARRY EMERSON FOSDICK

*T*he man or woman who turns to God is like a tree planted by a stream. What they share with the world is replenished from a source beyond themselves, so that they never run dry.

HAROLD KUSHNER

*G*od is our refuge and strength, a very present help in trouble.

PSALM 46:1

*T*he human soul never ceases to be modified by its encounter with might, swept on, blinded by that which it believes itself able to handle, bowed beneath the power of that which it suffers.

SIMONE WEIL

Suffering

God has given me the bread of adversity and the water of trouble.

ANNE ASKEW

Sorrow makes a man think of God.

PAUL BRUNTON

A man who was afflicted with a terrible disease complained to Rabbi Israel of Rizhyn that his suffering interfered with his learning and praying. The rabbi put his hand on his shoulder and said: "How do you know, friend, what is more pleasing to God, your studying or your suffering?"

MARTIN BUBER

No suffering befalls the man who calls nothing his own.

DHAMMAPADA

The hardest heart and the grossest ignorance must disappear before the rising sun of suffering without anger and without malice.

MOHANDAS K. GANDHI

Great grief is a divine and terrible radiance which transfigures the wretched.

VICTOR-MARIE HUGO

The more we are afflicted in this world, the greater is our assurance for the next; the more we sorrow in the present, the greater will be our joy in the future.

ST. ISIDORE OF SEVILLE

Suffering out of love of God is better than working miracles.

ST. JOHN OF THE CROSS

Affliction is able to drown out every earthly voice . . . but the voice of eternity within a man it cannot drown.

SØREN KIERKEGAARD

To grasp the thought of suffering, and the message of joy in suffering, to endure suffering and truly find good in it, to choose to suffer and believe that this is true wisdom unto blessedness, a man requires the guidance of God.

SØREN KIERKEGAARD

Sometimes I suspect that great art—music, painting, poetry—is only born out of great pain, the sort of pain that shatters your old world-view, and compels you to give birth to a new one.

HAROLD KUSHNER

Rabbi Alexandri said: "If a person uses broken vessels, it is considered an embarrassment. But God seeks out broken vessels for his use, as it says: 'God is the healer of shattered hearts.'"

LEVITICUS RABBAH

Some people feel guilty about their anxieties and regard them as a defeat of faith; they are afflictions, not sins. Like all afflictions, they are, if we can so take them, our share in the passion of Christ.

C. S. LEWIS

I do not believe that sheer suffering teaches. If suffering alone taught, all the world would be wise, since everyone suffers. To suffering must be added mourning, understanding, patience, love, opennness, and the willingness to remain vulnerable.

ANNE MORROW LINDBERGH

*T*he more Christian a man is, the more evils, sufferings, and deaths he must endure.

MARTIN LUTHER

*O*n the wintry landscape, the searcher hears psalms sung, sees pilgrim bands, smells the incense of restored prayer, touches the company of the faithful, and even tastes.

MARTIN E. MARTY

*S*uffering, as both Christianity and Buddhism see, each in its own way, is part of our ego-identity and empirical existence, and the only thing to do about it is to plunge right into the middle of contradiction and confusion in order to be transformed by what Zen calls the "Great Death" and Christianity calls "dying and rising with Christ."

THOMAS MERTON

*N*othing is ever suffered in plural. There is only one body. Only one death.

STEPHEN MITCHELL

*M*en are tormented by the opinions they have of things, not by the things themselves.

MICHEL DE MONTAIGNE

*E*arth has no sorrow that Heaven cannot heal.

THOMAS MORE

*U*nless we agree to suffer we cannot be free from suffering.

D. T. SUZUKI

*W*e always find that those who walked closest to Christ Our Lord were those we had to bear the greatest trials.

ST. TERESA OF AVILA

*S*uffering is the substance of life and the root of personality, for it is only suffering that makes us persons.

MIGUEL DE UNAMUNO Y JUGO

*N*o Christian escapes a taste of the wilderness on the way to the Promised Land.

EVELYN UNDERHILL

*A*nyone that suffers is God's representative.

SWAMI VIVEKANANDA

*E*ven the most skeptical cling to the aesthetics, the history of Orthodoxy, until in a crisis, whether some personal quarrel or national disaster, the blood and tears of faith come pouring out.

PATRICK WHITE

*C*lergymen and people who use phrases without wisdom sometimes talk of suffering as a mystery. It is really a revelation. One discerns things one never discerned before.

OSCAR WILDE

Where anguish is greatest, the religious message is most significant. If God does not speak to suffering, to the shattered hearts of the Psalmist's plea, then he must remain peripheral to our lives.

DAVID WOLPE

Theology

A theology—any theology—not based on a spiritual experience is mere panting—religious breathlessness.

LEONARDO BOFF

*T*heology . . . is a discourse both intimate and public.

CHUNG HYUN KYUNG

*W*hat matters is the coming to awareness of millions of people who once believed the squalor they lived in was decreed by fate or willed by God but have now begun to know themselves as coworkers with God in the shaping of the future: what matters is not theology, but liberation.

HARVEY COX

I have only a small flickering light to guide me in the darkness of a thick forest. Up comes a theologian and blows it out.

DENIS DIDEROT

*T*he cure for false theology is motherwit. Forget your books and traditions, and obey your moral perceptions at this hour.

RALPH WALDO EMERSON

*I*n order to keep our theology supple and responsive to individual differences and changes, we must remember that all theology—all thinking about deities and godly powers—is done by individual people in particular situations.

NAOMI R. GOLDENBERG

*T*heology is an attempt to explain a subject by men who do not understand it. The intent is not to tell the truth but to satisfy the questioner.

ELBERT HUBBARD

*I*n theology the great man recoils at the thought of dogmatism, for he knows its vanity.

HYPATIA

*T*he point is, could God pass an examination in Theology?

MALCOLM MUGGERIDGE

Tolerance

*T*oleration is good for all, or it is good for none.

EDMUND BURKE

*I*n the practice of tolerance, one's enemy is the best teacher.

FOURTEENTH DALAI LAMA

*T*olerance grows only when faith loses certainty; certainty is murderous.

WILL & ARIEL DURANT

*L*ike the bee gathering honey from different flowers, the wise man accepts the essence of different Scriptures and sees only the good in all religions.

SRIMAD BHAGAVATAM

*W*hat is toleration? It is the appurtenance of humanity. We are all full of weakness and errors; let us mutually pardon each other our follies—it is the first law of nature.

VOLTAIRE

*T*he longer I live, the larger allowances I make for human infirmities.

JOHN WESLEY

Torah

The Torah is the tool of the Creator; with it and for it He created the universe. The Torah is older than creation. It is the highest idea and the living soul of the world.

HAYIM NAHMAN BIALIK

[In the Pentateuch] God pokes his nose into all the nooks and crannies of life. There are laws about birds' nests, and shopping-scales, infectious diseases and care of the environment.

LIONEL BLUE

Turn it, and turn it, for everything is in it.

PIRKE AVOT

Jewish feminists, in other words, must reclaim Torah as our own. We must render visible the presence, experience and deeds of women erased in traditional sources.

JUDITH PLASKOW

Truth

The truth that makes men free is for the most part the truth which men prefer not to hear.

HERBERT AGAR

There is a tragic clash between Truth and the world. Pure undistorted Truth burns up the world.

NIKOLAY BERDYAYEV

Those who know the truth are not equal to those who love it.

CONFUCIUS

If men can ever learn to accept their truths as not final, and if they can ever learn to build on something better than dogma, they may not be found saying, discouragedly, every once in so often, that every civilization carries in it the seeds of decay.

CLARENCE SHEPARD DAY, JR.

If God were able to backslide from truth I would fain cling to truth and let God go.

MEISTER ECKHART

I cannot prove scientifically that truth must be conceived as a truth that is valid independent of humanity; but I believe it firmly.

ALBERT EINSTEIN

*T*he ultimate aim of the human mind, in all its efforts, is to become acquainted with Truth.

ELIZA FARNHAM

*E*motionalism never finds depths of truth, but depth of truth cannot be had apart from a full and free emotional response.

NELS FERRE

*T*here is no God higher than Truth.

MOHANDAS K. GANDHI

*T*he true is Godlike: we do not see it itself; we guess at it through its manifestations.

J. W. VON GOETHE

*I*f you continue in my word, you are truly my disciples, and you will know the truth, and the truth will make you free.

JOHN 8:31–32

*I*t does not require many words to speak the truth.

CHIEF JOSEPH

*T*he smallest atom of truth represents some man's bitter toil and agony; for every ponderable chunk of it there is a brave truth-seeker's grave upon some lonely ash-dump and a soul roasting in hell.

H. L. MENCKEN

*W*e spend all our time looking for some concept of Truth, but Truth is what is left when we drop all concepts.

DAVID MERZEL

*R*eligious truth is not only a presentation, but a condition of general knowledge.

JOHN HENRY NEWMAN

*T*ruth is the beginning of every good thing, both in Heaven and on earth; and he who would be blessed and happy should be from the first a partaker of the truth, for then he can be trusted.

PLATO

*W*e move closer to the truth only to the extent that we move further from life.

SOCRATES

*M*an may burn his brother at the stake, but he cannot reduce truth to ashes; he may murder his fellow man with a shot in the back, but he does not murder justice; he may slay armies of men, but as it is written, "Truth bearest off the victory."

ADLAI E. STEVENSON

*O*urs is an age in which partial truths are tirelessly transformed into total falsehoods and then acclaimed as revolutionary revelations.

THOMAS SZASZ

*T*he false can never grow into truth by growing into power.

RABINDRANATH TAGORE

Unity/The Way/Oneness

*W*e are part of one great Life, which knows no failure, no loss of effort or strength, which "mightily and sweetly ordering all things" bears the worlds onwards to their goal.

ANNIE BESANT

*I*f the doors of perception were cleansed everything would appear to man as it is, infinite.

WILLIAM BLAKE

I cannot affirm God if I do not affirm man. If I deny the oneness of man, I deny the oneness of God. Therefore I affirm both. Without a belief in human unity, I am hungry and incomplete.

NORMAN COUSINS

*T*he iron walls of the self may be torn down in a magnificent triumph of common purpose and common conscience as men discover they are but single cells in a larger and common body.

NORMAN COUSINS

*T*he human race is most like unto God when it is most one, for the principle of unity dwells in him alone.

DANTE

*M*editate on Oneness. Release the small self to the Infinite, and the Infinite will take care of itself.

VIMALIA MCCLURE

I have put duality away, I have seen that the two worlds are one: One I seek, One I know, One I see, One I call. He is the first, he is the last. He is the outward, he is the inward.

JALĀL AD-DĪN AR-RŪMĪ

*J*oy is the realization of oneness, the oneness of our soul with the world and of the world–soul with the supreme love.

RABINDRANATH TAGORE

*W*ithout the slightest doubt *there is something* through which material and spiritual energy hold together and are complementary. In the last analysis, *somehow or other,* there must be a single energy operating in the world.

PIERRE TEILHARD DE CHARDIN

I now understand that my welfare is only possible if I acknowledge my unity with all the people of the world without exception.

LEO TOLSTOY

*O*M! This syllable is the whole world. Its further explanation is: the past, the present, the future—Everything is just the word OM.

UPANISHADS

*Y*ou are a part of the Infinite. This is your nature. Hence you are your brother's keeper.

SWAMI VIVEKANANDA

Violence & Nonviolence

*F*or this reason was the human created alone, to teach that whoever destroys a single soul of Israel, Scripture considers it as if he had destroyed the whole world.

BABYLONAN TALMUD

*H*e, who seeking his own happiness punishes or kills beings who also long for happiness, will not find happiness after death.

DHAMMAPADA

I object to violence because when it appears to do good, the good is only temporary; the evil it does is permanent.

MOHANDAS K. GANDHI

*H*e who believes in non-violence believes in a living God.

MOHANDAS K. GANDHI

*A*t the center of non-violence stands the principle of love.

MARTIN LUTHER KING, JR.

*I*t is no longer a choice between violence and nonviolence in this world, it's nonviolence or nonexistence.

MARTIN LUTHER KING, JR.

*O*nly the Supreme Executioner kills. To kill in place of the Supreme Executioner is to hack in place of a great carpenter. Now if one hacks in place of a great carpenter one can scarcely avoid cutting one's hand.

LAO-TZU

*M*uch violence is based on the illusion that life is a property to be defended and not to be shared.

HENRI NOUWEN

*I*f you wish to be brothers, let the arms fall from your hands. One cannot love while holding offensive arms.

POPE PIUS VI

War & Peace

The most disadvantageous peace is better than the most just war.

DESIDERIUS ERASMUS

War will hit you hard
Coming at you like lions raging.

HIND BINT UTBA

And they shall beat their swords into plowshares,
and their spears into pruning hooks;
nation shall not lift up sword against nation,
neither shall they learn war any more.

ISAIAH 2:4

Peace is not just the absence of war. . . . Like a cathedral,
peace must be constructed patiently and with unshakable faith.

POPE JOHN PAUL II

All men desire peace, but few desire the things that make for peace.

THOMAS À KEMPIS

*T*he past is prophetic in that it asserts loudly that wars are poor chisels for carving out peaceful tomorrows. One day we must come to see that peace is not merely a distant goal that we seek, but a means by which we arrive at that goal.

MARTIN LUTHER KING, JR.

*B*lessed are the peacemakers, for they shall be called sons of God.

MATTHEW 5:9

*B*ecause peace, like the kingdom of God itself, is both a divine gift and a human work, the Church should continually pray for the gift and share in the work.

PASTORAL LETTER OF THE NATIONAL CATHOLIC BISHOPS
ON WAR AND PEACE

*I*ndeed, the olive branch of peace can never blossom when human stems are dried and branches withered.

WILLIAM R. TOLBERT, JR.

Wisdom

*W*hen the stomach speaks wisdom is silent.

ARAB PROVERB

*A*ll wisdom may be reduced to two words—wait and hope.

ALEXANDRE DUMAS

*B*efore God we are all equally wise and equally foolish.

ALBERT EINSTEIN

*O*ne of the tendencies of our age is to use children's suffering to discredit the goodness of God. In this popular pity, we mark our gain in sensibility and our loss in vision. If other ages felt less, they saw more.

FLANNERY O'CONNOR

*T*o be brave in misfortune is to be worthy of manhood; to be wise in misfortune is to conquer fate.

AGNES REPPLIER

*S*cience says: "We must live," and seeks the means of prolonging, increasing, facilitating, and amplifying life, of making it tolerable and acceptable; wisdom says: "We must die," and seeks how to make us die well.

MIGUEL DE UNAMUNO Y JUGO

World & Universe

*C*ease not to think of the Universe as one living Being, possessed of a single Substance and a single soul.

MARCUS AURELIUS

*T*his external universe is a cinema show to the realised Man. It is free and the performance goes on day and night! He lives and works in it knowing that its objects and bodies (persons) are illusionary appearances just as an ordinary man knows the scenes and characters on the cinema screen at a theatre are illusions and do not exist in real life.

PAUL BRUNTON

*W*hen we once understood that the universe is a great smelting-pot, and the Creator a great founder, where can we go that will not be right?

CHUANG-TZU

*F*ather, we thank you, especially for letting me fly this flight . . . for the privilege of being able to be in this position, to be in this wondrous place, seeing all these many startling, wonderful things that you have created.

GORDON COOPER (WHILE ORBITING THE EARTH)

I may not embrace or command this universal order, but I can be at one with it, for I am of it.

NORMAN COUSINS

I would rather live in a world where my life is surrounded by mystery than live in a world so small that my mind could comprehend it.

HARRY EMERSON FOSDICK

I realize that we are only throwaway, that we've never designed anything, that the universe exhibits a mathematical orderliness which naturally implies a greater intellect at work, and that we are part of that design.

R. BUCKMINSTER FULLER

*A*t bottom the whole concern of both morality and religion is with the manner of our acceptance of the universe.

WILLIAM JAMES

I can see, and that is why I can be happy, in what you call the dark, but which to me is golden. I can see a God-made world, not a man-made world.

HELEN KELLER

*I*f the universe is so bad, or even half so bad, how on earth did human beings ever come to attribute it to the activity of a wise and good Creator?

C. S. LEWIS

*W*e alone can—like God–mother—love and befriend the world, the body that God has made available to us as both the divine presence and our home.

SALLIE MCFAGUE

*T*he plots of God are perfect. The Universe is a plot of God.

EDGAR ALLEN POE

The entire universe, as I see it, is the outward manifestation of Mind Energy, of spirit, or to use the older and better word, of God.

MILTON STEINBERG

The stuff of the universe, woven in a single piece according to one and the same system but never repeating itself from one point to another, represents a single figure. Structurally it forms a Whole.

PIERRE TEILHARD DE CHARDIN

Each creature is most fully that which it is created to be, an almost incredible reflection of the infinite, the invisible, the indefinable. All women and men participate in that reflected glory.

DESMOND TUTU

Worship

*W*onder is the basis of Worship.

THOMAS CARLYLE

*A*mong men there is no nation so savage and ferocious as to deny the necessity of worshipping God, however ignorant it may be respecting the nature of his attributes.

CICERO

*T*he simplest person, who in his integrity worships God, becomes God.

RALPH WALDO EMERSON

*P*erfect human joy is also worship, for it is ordered by God.

FRIEDRICH FROEBEL

*W*hen the worshipper no longer thinks of his worship or himself but is altogether absorbed in Him whom he worships, that state is called *fana* (extinction).

ABU-HĀMID MUHAMMAD AL-GHAZĀLĪ

*W*orship is a way of living, a way of seeing the world in the light of God. To worship is to rise to a higher level of existence, to see the world from the point of view of God.

ABRAHAM JOSHUA HESCHEL

*W*orship liberates when it is lived in truthfulness before God, but it alienates when it is limited to a sacral world, a world apart, in the belief that we can approach God even though we neglect the concrete practice of love for our fellow human beings.

BAKOLE WA ILUNGA

*L*et us worship God again in simplicity, instead of making a fool of him in splendid edifices.

SØREN KIERKEGAARD

*W*hen someone says, "Oh, I can worship God anywhere," the answer is, "Do you?"

JAMES PIKE

*T*he test of worship is how far it makes us *more sensitive* to "the beyond in our midst," to the Christ in the hungry, the naked, the homeless and the prisoner.

J. A. T. ROBINSON

Appendix

Source Descriptions

Below is a list of brief descriptions of selected people and texts quoted in this book.

A

Aba Saiid Ibn Abi Khayr, eleventh-century Persian Sufi mystic

Peter Abelard, eleventh- and twelfth-century French philosopher and lover of Héloise

Herbert Agar, twentieth-century American journalist

Robert Aitken, twentieth-century American astronomer

John M. Allin, twentieth-century English Church of England theologian

Saint Ambrose, fourth-century Italian Bishop of Milan

Henri Frederic Amiel, nineteenth-century Swiss philosopher and author

Anandamayi Ma, twentieth-century Bangladeshi Hindu spiritual leader

Jean Anouilh, twentieth-century French dramatist

Minna Antrim, nineteenth- and twentieth-century American author

Apollonius of Tyana, first-century Greek philosopher and seer

Saint Thomas Aquinas, thirteenth-century Italian scholastic philosopher and theologian

Hannah Arendt, twentieth-century German-American philosopher and political theorist

Aristides, second-century Greek Christian apologist

Arjan, sixteenth-century Iranian fifth Guru of the Sikhs

Matthew Arnold, nineteenth-century English poet and critic

Sholem Asch, twentieth-century Polish Yiddish playwright and novelist

Anne Askew, sixteenth-century English Protestant martyr
Saint Athanasius (of Alexandria), fourth-century Greek theologian
Saint Augustine, third-century Christian philosopher
Marcus Aurelius, second-century Roman emperor and Stoic philosopher
Sri Aurobindo (Ghose) nineteenth- and twentieth-century Indian philosopher, poet, and mystic

B

Maltbie D. Babcock, nineteenth-century American Presbyterian minister and author
Babylonian Talmud, classic literature of rabbinic Judaism
Leo Baeck, twentieth-century German Jewish religious leader
Bahaullah (or Bahā' Allāh), nineteenth-century Persian religious leader and founder of the Bahā'ī faith
Pearl Bailey, twentieth-century American jazz singer
James Baldwin, twentieth-century American author
Djuna Barnes, twentieth-century American author and illustrator
Karl Barth, twentieth-century Swiss theologian
Bashō (Matsuo Munefusa), seventeenth-century Japanese poet and mystic
Diana Baskin, twentieth-century Amerian author on Hinduism
P. N. Basu, twentieth-century scholar of Indian religions
Baudonivia, sixth-century Christian mystic
Simone de Beauvior, twentieth-century French writer and philosopher
Henry Ward Beecher, nineteenth-century American Congregationalist clergy
William Bennett, twentieth-century American Secretary of Department of Education
Robert Hugh Benson, nineteenth- and twentieth-century English Roman Catholic priest and novelist
Nikolay Berdyayev, twentieth-century Russian religious philosopher
Henri-Louis Bergson, nineteenth- and twentieth-century French philosopher
Georges Bernanos, twentieth-century French author
Saint Bernard of Clairvaux, twelfth-century French ecclesiastic
Daniel Berrigan, twentieth-century American Catholic priest and peace activist
Annie Besant, nineteenth- and twentieth-century English theosophist and social reformer
Bhagavad-Gita, B.C.E. third- to sixth-century Sanskrit poem within the sacred Hindu text *Mahabharata*

Hayim Nahman Bialik, twentieth-century Hebrew man of letters

Ambrose Bierce, nineteenth-century American journalist and humorist

Chief Big Elk (Ongpatonga, Om-Dah-Ton-Ga), eighteenth- and nineteenth-century Native American Chief of the Omahas

William Blake, eighteenth- and nineteenth-century English poet, painter, engraver, and mystic

Ann Eliza Bleecker, eighteenth-century American poet

Lionel Blue, twentieth-century British author and rabbi

Bodhisattva Amitabha, celestial buddha venerated by Pureland sect of Buddhism

Jakob Boehme, sixteenth-century German theosopist

Leonardo Boff, twentieth-century Brazilian Franciscan liberation theologian

Ben Zion Bokser, twentieth-century American Conservative rabbi and scholar

Robert Bolt, twentieth-century English playwright and film director

Dietrich Bonhoeffer, twentieth-century German Lutheran pastor and theologian

Book of the Dead, ancient Tibetan Buddhist text

Daniel Boorstin, twentieth-century American historian

Margaret Bourke-White, twentieth-century American photojournalist

Malcolm Boyd, twentieth-century American author and social commentator

Omar Bradley, twentieth-century American military general and chair of Joint Chiefs of Staff

Louis Brandeis, nineteenth- and twentieth-century American jurist and United States Supreme Court Justice

G. Brenan, twentieth-century English travel writer and novelist

Phillips Brooks, nineteenth-century American Protestant Episcopal bishop

Robert McAfee Brown, twentieth-century American Christian theologian and minister

Thomas Browne, Sir, seventeenth-century English author and physician

Elizabeth Barrett Browning, nineteenth-century English poet

Lenny Bruce, twentieth-century American comedian and satirist

Emil Brunner, twentieth-century Swiss Reformed theologian

Paul Brunton, twentieth-century American philosopher of Eastern religion

William Jennings Bryan, nineteenth- and twentieth-century American jurist and politician

Martin Buber, twentieth-century German Jewish theologian

Pearl S. Buck, twentieth-century American author

Buddha (Siddhārtha Guatama), B.C.E. sixth- and fifth-century founder of Buddhism

Frederick Buechner, twentieth-century American Presbyterian minister and author

Rudolf Bultmann, twentieth-century German Protestant theologian

Anthony Burgess, twentieth-century English novelist, critic, and composer

Edmund Burke, eighteenth-century Irish politician, statesman, and philosopher

John Burroughs, nineteenth-century American naturalist and author

Vannevar Bush, twentieth-century American electrical engineer and inventor

Samuel Butler, seventeenth-century English satirist

C

Caecilius, B.C.E. first-century Roman comedist

Ernest Campbell, twentieth-century American professor of sociology

Albert Camus, twentieth-century French philosopher and author

Katie G. Cannon, twentieth-century African-American Christian feminist theologian

Thomas Carlyle, nineteenth-century English historian and essayist

Willa Cather, nineteenth-century American novelist

Catherine of Siena (Saint Catherine), fourteenth-century Italian mystic

David Cecil, Lord, twentieth-century English literary critic and biographer

Miguel de Cervantes, sixteenth- and seventeenth-century Spanish author of the first novel

Satis Bankim Chatterjee, nineteenth-century Indian author

G. K. Chesterton, nineteenth-century English critic, novelist, and poet

Lydia M. Child, nineteenth-century American abolitionist and author

John Chrysostom (Saint John), fourth-century Greek Eastern church father and bishop

Chuang-Tzu, B.C.E. fourth- to third-century ancient Chinese thinker

Chung Hyun Kyung, twentieth-century Korean feminist theologian

Winston Churchill, twentieth-century English statesman and prime minister

Cicero, B.C.E. first-century Roman orator, statesman, and writer

Saint Clement of Alexandria, third-century Greek theologian

Jean Cocteau, twentieth-century French poet, playwright, and film director

Henry Sloane Coffin, twentieth-century American Presbyterian minister and theologian

William Sloane Coffin, twentieth-century American minister and theologian

Samuel Taylor Coleridge, eighteenth- and nineteenth-century English poet

Sheila Collins, twentieth-century American religious scholar

C. C. Colton, eighteenth- and nineteenth-century English clergy and author

James Cone, twentieth-century African-American theologian

Confucius (K'ung Fu-tzu), B.C.E. sixth- and fifth-century Chinese philosopher

Joseph Conrad, nineteenth- and twentieth-century English novelist

Gordon Cooper, twentieth-century American astronaut

Norman Cousins, twentieth-century American author and editor

Paul Cowan, twentieth-century American Jewish author

Abraham Cowley, seventeenth-century English poet

William Cowper, eighteenth-century English poet

Harvey Cox, twentieth-century American theologian

Richard Cardinal Cushing, twentieth-century American Roman Catholic archbishop of Boston

Saint Cyril of Jerusalem, second-century Catholic ecclasiastic of Alexandria

D

Fourteenth Dalai Lama (Tenzin Gyatso), twentieth-century Tibetan Buddhist spiritual leader

Mary Daly, twentieth-century American feminist theologian and philosopher

Dante, thirteenth- and fourteenth-century Italian poet

Elizabeth Gould Davis, twentieth-century American feminist author

Clarence Shepard Day, Jr., nineteenth- and twentieth-century American author

Dorothy Day, twentieth-century American social reformer and cofounder of the Catholic Worker Movement

Vine Deloria, Jr., twentieth-century Native American author

John Dewey, twentieth-century American philosopher and educator

Dhammapada, fifth-century Buddhist text

Emily Dickinson, nineteenth-century American poet

Denis Diderot, eighteenth-century French author

Annie Dillard, twentieth-century American author

Benjamin Disraeli, nineteenth-century English statesman and novelist

John Donne, sixteenth- and seventeenth-century English poet
Fyodor Dostoyevski, nineteenth-century Russian author
Thomas Draxe, seventeenth-century English preacher
Theodore Dreiser, nineteenth- and twentieth-century American novelist
John Dryden, seventeenth-century English poet
Alexandre Dumas, nineteenth-century French novelist and playwright
Will and Ariel Durant, twentieth-century American historians

E

Amelia Earhart, twentieth-century American aviator
Charles Alexander Eastman, nineteenth- and twentieth-century Native American physician
Meister Eckhart, thirteenth- and fourteenth-century German mystic
Mary Baker Eddy, nineteenth-century American clergy and founder of the Christian Science Church
Marian Wright Edelman, twentieth-century African-American social reformer
Jonathan Edwards, eighteenth-century American philosopher and theologian
Albert Einstein, twentieth-century German-American scientist
Mircea Eliade, twentieth-century Romanian historian and religious scholar
George Eliot, nineteenth-century English novelist
Ralph Waldo Emerson, nineteenth-century American philosopher and poet
Epictetus, first- and second-century Greek Stoic philosopher and moralist
Desiderius Erasmus, fifteenth- and sixteenth-century Dutch humanist and scholar

F

Clifton Fadiman, twentieth-century American writer and editor
Eliza Farnham, nineteenth-century American philanthropist and author
Walter Farrell, author of *My Way of Life*, 1952
Millicent Garrett Fawcett, nineteenth- and twentieth-century English suffragist and proponent of educational reform
Owen Felltham, seventeenth-century English author
François Fénelon, seventeenth- and eighteenth-century French prelate and author
Nels Ferre, twentieth-century Swedish-American Congregational minister

Geoffrey Fisher, nineteenth-century English prelate and archbishop of Canterbury

Harry Emerson Fosdick, nineteenth- and twentieth-century American Baptist minister

Matthew Fox, twentieth-century American priest and theologian

Saint Francis of Sales, sixteenth- and seventeenth-century French nobleman and ecclesiastic

Benjamin Franklin, eighteenth-century American statesman and inventor

Friedrich Froebel, nineteenth-century German educator and founder of the kindergarten system

Erich Fromm, twentieth-century American psychoanalyst and social philosopher

Robert Fulghum, twentieth-century American author

R. Buckminster Fuller, twentieth-century American inventor

G

Galileo, sixteenth- and seventeenth-century Italian astronomer, mathematician, and natural philosopher

George Gallup, twentieth-century American pollster

Mohandas K. Gandhi, twentieth-century Indian nationalist and leader of the nonviolent movement

Harold Gardiner, twentieth-century American author

Charles Garman, nineteenth-century American philosophy scholar

Sally Gearhart, twentieth-century American author

Henry George, nineteenth-century American economist

Abu-Hāmid Muhammad al-Ghazālī, eleventh- and twelfth-century Muslim philosopher and mystic

Kahlil Gibran, nineteenth-century Syrian symbolist poet and painter

André Gide, nineteenth-century French novelist and diarist

Eric Gill, twentieth-century English sculptor, engraver, writer, and typographer

J. W. von Goethe, eighteenth- and nineteenth-century German poet, dramatist, scientist, and court official

Isaac Goldberg, nineteenth- and twentieth-century Israeli Zionist leader

Naomi R. Goldenberg, twentieth-century Jewish feminist theologian

Ari Goldman, twentieth-century American religion writer and journalist

Stephen Jay Gould, twentieth-century American biologist
Billy Graham, twentieth-century American evangelist
Graham Greene, twentieth-century English author
Saint Gregory the Great, sixth-century Roman prefect and pope
Bede Griffiths, twentieth-century writer on Hindu-Christian dialogue
Angelina Grimké, nineteenth-century American abolitionist
Gustavo Gutierrez, twentieth-century Peruvian liberation theologian/
   philosopher

H

Shaykh Fadhlella Haeri, twentieth-century Islamic teacher and author
Judah Halevi, eleventh- and twelfth-century Spanish Jewish poet and phi-
   losopher
Edith Hamilton, twentieth-century American historian and scholar
Ahmad Zak Hammad, twentieth-century Egyptian-American Islamic law
   scholar
Dag Hammarskjöld, twentieth-century Swedish statesman and United Na-
   tions secretary general
Knut Hamsun, nineteenth- and twentieth-century Norwegian novelist
Jane Ellen Harrison, nineteenth- and twentieth-century English classical
   scholar
Hassan II, twentieth-century Morrocan monarch
Joseph Haydn, eighteenth-century Austrian composer
G. W. F. Hegel, nineteenth-century German philosopher
Heinrich Heine, nineteenth-century German poet and essayist
Lillian Hellman, twentieth-century American playwright
Héloise, twelfth-century French abbess
Heraclitus, B.C.E. sixth- and fifth-century Greek philosopher
Will Herberg, twentieth-century American scholar and author
Arthur Hertzberg, twentieth-century American Conservative rabbi and au-
   thor
Abraham Joshua Heschel, twentieth-century American Jewish religious phi-
   losopher
Carter Heyward, twentieth-century American feminist theologian
Joel Hildebrand, twentieth-century American chemist
Hildegard of Bingen, eleventh- and twelfth-century German nun, scholar,
   and mystic

Hillel, B.C.E. first-century Babylonian Jewish sage

Hind bint Utba, seventh-century Indian politician, soldier, and mother of Mu'awiya

John Haynes Holmes, twentieth-century American Unitarian minister and author

Oliver Wendell Holmes, twentieth-century American jurist and Supreme Court Justice

Barry Holtz, twentieth-century American Jewish educator

Homer, B.C.E. ninth- and eighth-century Greek epic poet

Gerard Manley Hopkins, nineteenth-century English Catholic priest and poet

Horace, B.C.E. first-century Roman poet and satirist

Edgar Watson Howe, nineteenth- and twentieth-century American journalist and author

Elbert Hubbard, nineteenth-century American writer, editor, and printer

Victor-Marie Hugo, nineteenth-century French novelist and poet

David Hume, eighteenth-century Scottish philosopher and historian

Aldous Huxley, twentieth-century English novelist and essayist; brother of Julian Huxley

Julian Huxley, Sir, twentieth-century biologist and humanist

Hypatia, fourth- and fifth-century Greek philosopher, astronomer, and mathematician

I

Saint Ignatius of Antioch, second-century Christian martyr

Saint Ignatius of Loyola, sixteenth-century Spanish soldier and ecclesiastic

Bakole wa Ilunga, twentieth-century Zairian Roman Catholic Archbishop

William Ralph Inge, twentieth-century English prelate and theologian

Eugène Ionesco, twentieth-century Romanian-born French playwright

Saint Isadore of Seville, sixth-century Spanish prelate and scholar

Israel ben Eliezer (Ba'al Shem Tov), eighteenth-century Polish founder of Hasidic movement

J

Jaina Sutras, B.C.E. sixth- to third-century ancient Hindu aphoristic manual

Jalāl ad-Dīn ar-Rūmī, thirteenth-century Persian poet and mystic

William James, nineteenth-century American philosopher and psychologist

Edward Jeffrey, twentieth-century English clergyman

Thomas Jefferson, eighteenth-century American statesman and third president of the United States

Saint Jerome, fourth- and fifth-century Latin Christian church father and biblical interpreter

Pope John XXIII, twentieth-century Italian head of Catholic Church

Saint John of the Cross, sixteenth-century Spanish mystic and poet

Saint John of Damascene, eighth-century Syrian church father and theologian

Pope John Paul II, twentieth-century Polish head of Catholic Church

Samuel Johnson, eighteenth-century English writer, critic, and lexicographer

William Johnston, twentieth-century Irish Jesuit and oriental studies scholar

Rufus M. Jones, twentieth-century American Quaker author

Chief Joseph (Hinmaton-Yalaktit), nineteenth-century Native American Chief of the Nez Perce

Morris Joseph, twentieth-century English Reform rabbi and author

Joseph Joubert, eighteenth-century French writer and moralist

Julian the Apostate, fourth-century Roman emperor

Julian of Norwich, fourteenth- and fifteenth-century English mystic

Carl Jung, nineteenth- and twentieth-century Swiss psychiatrist

Juvenal, first- and second-century Roman lawyer and satirist

K

Immanuel Kant, eighteenth-century German philosopher

Mordecai M. Kaplan, twentieth-century American Jewish thinker and founder of Reconstructionist Judaism

Nikos Kazantzakis, twentieth-century Greek novelist

Helen Keller, twentieth-century American author

Margery Kempe, fourteenth-century English mystic

Thomas à Kempis, fourteenth- and fifteenth-century Dutch religious writer

Jean Kerr, twentieth-century American author

Søren Kierkegaard, nineteenth-century Danish philosopher and religious thinker

C. H. Kilmer, author of *The New Illustrator*, 1945

Martin Luther King, Jr., twentieth-century American Baptist minister and civil rights leader

Ronald A. Knox, twentieth-century English Roman Catholic prelate and writer

Arthur Koestler, twentieth-century Hungarian English novelist

Kenneth Kramer, twentieth-century American religious scholar

Jiddu Krishnamurti, twentieth-century Indian theosophist

Harold Kushner, twentieth-century American rabbi and author

L

Lactantius, third- and fourth-century Christian apologist

Alphonse de Lamartine, nineteenth-century French poet, statesman, and historian

Sidney Lanier, nineteenth-century American poet

Lao-tzu, B.C.E. sixth-century Chinese philosopher

John E. Large, author of *The Small Needle of Doctor Large,* 1962

Francois de La Rochefoucauld, seventeenth-century French political author

William Law, eighteenth-century English devotional author

D. H. Lawrence, nineteenth- and twentieth-century English novelist

Bernard Lazare, nineteenth-century French author on anti-Semitism and Zionism

Stanislaw Lec, twentieth-century Polish poet

Moshe Leib, eighteenth-century Polish Hasidic teacher

G. W. Leibniz, seventeenth-century German philosopher and mathematician

Madeleine L'Engle, twentieth-century American author

C. S. Lewis, twentieth-century English author

Edwin Lewis, twentieth-century American psychologist

Joshua Loth Liebman, twentieth-century American rabbi and radio preacher

Anne Morrow Lindbergh, twentieth-century American author

Lin Yü-t'ang, twentieth-century Chinese author and philologist

Walter Lippmann, twentieth-century American journalist

Martyn Lloyd-Jones, twentieth-century Welsh preacher and author

Christine Longford, twentieth-century English countess and author

Henri de Lubac, twentieth-century French historian

John Lubbock, Sir, nineteenth-century English astronomer and mathematician

Jean Marie Cardinal Lustiger, twentieth-century French Roman Catholic prelate

Martin Luther, fifteenth- and sixteenth-century German religious reformer

M

George Macdonald, nineteenth-century Scottish novelist and poet
Archibald MacLeish, twentieth-century American poet
Jonathan Magonet, twentieth-century English reform rabbi
Nisaragada Ha Maharaj, twentieth-century Indian Hindu teacher
Moses Maimonides, twelfth-century Spanish rabbi and philosopher
Manu-Smirti, ancient Sanskrit Hindu law
Jacques Maritain, twentieth-century French philosopher
Peter Marshall, twentieth-century Scottish-born American Presbyterian
    clergyman and theologian
James A. Martin, Jr., twentieth-century American theologian and scholar
Harriett Martineau, nineteenth-century English novelist and economist
Martin E. Marty, twentieth-century American theologian
Karl Marx, nineteenth-century German-born English political philosopher
François Mauriac, twentieth-century French author
Vimalia McClure, twentieth-century American author
Sallie McFague, twentieth-century American theologian
William McGill, twentieth-century American psychologist and president of
    Columbia University
Phyllis McGinley, twentieth-century American poet and writer
Margaret Mead, twentieth-century American anthropologist
Herman Melville, nineteenth-century American novelist
Mencius (Meng-tzu), B.C.E. fourth- and third-century Chinese philosopher
H. L. Mencken, twentieth-century American journalist
Moses Mendelssohn, eighteenth-century German Jewish philosopher
Karl Menninger, twentieth-century American psychiatrist
Thomas Merton, twentieth-century American Trappist monk and philoso-
    pher
David Merzel, twentieth-century American author
Agnes Meyer, twentieth-century American journalist and social critic
Michelangelo, sixteenth-century Italian sculptor, painter, architect, and
    poet
Samuel Miller, nineteenth-century American jurist
A. A. Milne, nineteenth-century English author
John Milton, seventeenth-century English poet

Stephen Mitchell, twentieth-century American religious translator and author

Molière, seventeenth-century French playwright and actor

W. P. Montague, nineteenth- and twentieth-century American philosopher

Michel de Montaigne, sixteenth-century French essayist

C. G. Montefiore, nineteenth- and twentieth-century English Jewish cultural and religious leader

Maria Montessori, nineteenth- and twentieth-century Italian physician and educator

Thomas More, Sir, fifteenth- and sixteenth-century English statesman and author

John Morley, nineteenth- and twentieth-century English author

Robert Lee Morton, twentieth-century American educator and author

Malcolm Muggeridge, twentieth-century English journalist

Muhammad, sixth- and seventh-century Arabian prophet and founder of Islam

Harith ibn-Asad al-Muhasibi, ninth-century Arab Sufi teacher

Lewis Mumford, twentieth-century American philosopher and social critic

T. D. Munda, twentieth-century American Zen teacher and musician

Murasaki Shikibu, tenth-century Japanese courtier and author

N

Mohammed Naguib, twentieth-century Egyptian military officer, politician, and author

Nahman of Bratslav, eighteenth-century Hasidic leader

Nānak, fifteenth-century Indian religious leader and founder of Sikhism

John Navone, twentieth-century American Roman Catholic theologian and scholar

Maurice Nedoncelle, twentieth-century French author

Joseph Needham, twentieth-century English biochemist and historian of Chinese science

Andre Neher, twentieth-century French Jewish scholar and theologian

Jawaharlal Nehru, twentieth-century Indian national political leader and prime minister

John Henry Newman, nineteenth-century English theologian

John Newton, eighteenth-century English clergyman and hymn writer

Thomas Newton, eighteenth-century English religious philosopher

Reinhold Niebuhr, twentieth-century American scholar and theologian
Friedrich Nietzsche, nineteenth-century German philosopher
Swami Nikhilananda, twentieth-century Indian author and Yoga master
Anaïs Nin, twentieth-century French–American diarist
Henri Nouwen, twentieth-century French Roman Catholic theologian and
     psychologist

O

Joyce Carol Oates, twentieth-century American author
Carol Ochs, twentieth-century American philosopher
John A. O'Brien, twentieth-century American Roman Catholic priest and
     author
Flannery O'Connor, twentieth-century American novelist
Leo O'Donovan, twentieth-century American scholar
Laurence Olivier, twentieth-century English actor, director, and producer
L. S. S. O'Malley, nineteenth-century Irish historian
Eugene O'Neill, twentieth-century American playwright
J. Robert Oppenheimer, twentieth-century American nuclear physicist
Origen, second- and third-century Greek Christian writer and teacher
Max C. Otto, twentieth-century German-American philosopher and author
Ovid, first-century Roman poet

P

Kirby Page, twentieth-century American social evangelist and author
Thomas Paine, eighteenth-century author and pundit
Theodore Parker, nineteenth-century American Unitarian clergyman
Blaise Pascal, seventeenth-century French philosopher
Coventry Patmore, nineteenth-century English poet
Pope Paul VI, twentieth-century Italian head of Catholic Church
M. Scott Peck, twentieth-century American author and psychiatrist
Charles-Pierre Peguy, nineteenth-century French author
Jaroslav Pelikan, twentieth-century American scholar
William Penn, seventeenth-century American clergy and founder of Penn-
     sylvania colony
Philo Judaeus, first-century Jewish philosopher of Alexandria
Pablo Picasso, twentieth-century Spanish painter

Charles E. Pierce, twentieth-century American scholar
James Pike, twentieth-century American Episcopal bishop and theologian
Pope Pius VI, eighteenth-century Italian head of Catholic Church
Pope Pius XI, twentieth-century Italian head of Catholic Church
Max Planck, twentieth-century German physicist
Judith Plaskow, twentieth-century American Jewish feminist theologian
Plato, B.C.E. fifth- and fourth-century Greek philosopher
Edgar Allan Poe, nineteenth-century American author
Polybius, B.C.E. first-century Greek historian
Adam Clayton Powell, twentieth-century American clergy and United States congressman
J. D. Pratt, author of *Can We Keep the Faith?*, 1941

Q

Qur'ān, seventh-century sacred scripture of Islam

R

Savrepalli Radhakrishnan, twentieth-century English East Indian-born philosopher and educator
Sri Ramakrishna, twentieth-century Indian Hindu yogi
Michael Ramsey, twentieth-century English prelate and archbishop of Canterbury
Uta Ranke-Heinemann, twentieth-century German Christian feminist theologian
E. Recejac, nineteenth-century French mystic and author
Agnes Repplier, twentieth-century American author
J. A. T. Robinson, twentieth-century English Anglican prelate and theologian
Denis de Rougemont, twentieth-century Swiss organization executive, publisher, and author
Rosemary Radford Ruether, twentieth-century American scholar and theologian
Robert Runcie, twentieth-century English prelate and archbishop of Canterbury
John Ruskin, nineteenth-century English art critic and sociological writer
Bertrand Russell, nineteenth-century English philosopher and mathematician

S

Vita Sackville-West, nineteenth-century English author

Carl Sagan, twentieth-century American astronomer

Antoine de Saint-Exupéry, twentieth-century French aviator and writer

Saki (Hector Hugh Munro), nineteenth-century Scottish author

Robert Sanchez, twentieth-century American author

George Sand, nineteenth-century French author

James A. Sanders, twentieth-century American biblical scholar

George Santayana, nineteenth- and twentieth-century American poet and
    philosopher

Sappho, B.C.E. sixth-century Greek poet

D. S. Sarma, twentieth-century Indian scholar and author

May Sarton, twentieth-century American author

Jean-Paul Sartre, twentieth-century French author and philosopher

Dorothy Sayers, twentieth-century English historian and mystery author

Francis B. Sayre, twentieth-century American lawyer and administrator

Jonathan Schell, twentieth-century American author

Arthur Schopenhauer, nineteenth-century German philosopher

Albert Schweitzer, twentieth-century German physician and biblical schol-
    ar

Elizabeth M. Scott, twentieth-century English author

Chief Seattle, nineteenth-century Native American chief of the Suquamish
    tribe

Seneca, first-century Roman rhetorician

William Shakespeare, sixteenth- and seventeenth-century English play-
    wright

George Bernard Shaw, nineteenth- and twentieth-century Irish playwright
    and philosopher

Fulton Sheen, twentieth-century American Roman Catholic prelate

Percy Bysshe Shelley, nineteenth-century English poet

Abba Hillel Silver, twentieth-century American rabbi and Zionist leader

Isaac Bashevis Singer, twentieth-century Polish-born American Yiddish author

Edmund Sinnott, twentieth-century American educator and botanist

Elizabeth Oakes Smith, nineteenth-century American author

Lillian Smith, twentieth-century American author

Wilfred C. Smith, twentieth-century Canadian theologian

Socrates, B.C.E. fifth- to fourth-century Greek philosopher

Sophocles, third-century Greek tragic playwright

Baruch Spinoza, seventeenth-century Dutch philosopher

Chief Luther Standing Bear, nineteenth- and twentieth-century Native American actor, lecturer, and author

Elizabeth Cady Stanton, nineteenth-century American suffragist

Starhawk (Miriam Simos), twentieth-century American feminist thinker

Douglas V. Steere, twentieth-century American theologian

Milton Steinberg, twentieth-century American rabbi and author

Gloria Steinem, twentieth-century American feminist and author

Adlai E. Stevenson, twentieth-century American politician

Harriet Beecher Stowe, nineteenth-century American author

Igor Stravinsky, twentieth-century Russian composer

Subhadra, Bhikshu, eighteenth- and nineteenth-century Buddhist teacher

Billy Sunday, nineteenth-century American evangelist

D. T. Suzuki, twentieth-century Japanese educator, philosopher, and author

Donald Swan, twentieth-century Welsh composer and lyricist

Publilus Syrus, B.C.E. first-century Roman playwright

Thomas Szasz, twentieth-century Hungarian-born American psychiatrist

T

Rabindranath Tagore, nineteenth-century Indian Bengali poet

Tao Te Ching, B.C.E. sixth- to fifth-century Chinese Taoist text

Pierre Teilhard de Chardin, twentieth-century French paleontologist and theologian

Merrill C. Tenney, twentieth-century American theologian

Mother Teresa, twentieth-century Albanian Loreto nun and poverty worker in Calcutta

Saint Teresa of Avila, sixteenth-century Spanish Carmelite nun and mystic

Tertullian, second- and third-century N. African (Latin) Christian author

Theophan the Recluse, eighth-century Christian chronicler of Constantinople

Bruce Thielemann, twentieth-century American Presbyterian minister

Barbara Thiering, twentieth-century Australian scholar

Dylan Thomas, twentieth-century English poet

Edith Thomas, nineteenth- and twentieth-century American poet

Norman Thomas, twentieth-century American socialist politician

Henry David Thoreau, nineteenth-century American philosopher and author

Lionel Tiger, twentieth-century Canadian sociologist and anthropologist

Paul Tillich, twentieth-century German-American Lutheran theologian and philosopher

William R. Tolbert, Jr., twentieth-century President of the Republic of Liberia

Melvin B. Tolson, twentieth-century American journalist and poet

Leo Tolstoy, nineteenth-century Russian author, philosopher, and social critic

Arnold J. Toynbee, nineteenth-century English sociologist and economist

Gerald C. Treacy, author of *The Devil*, 1952

George M. Trevelyan, nineteenth-century English historian

Tripitaka, B.C.E. first-century three-part collection of sacred Buddhist writings

D. E. Trueblood, twentieth-century American Quaker scholar

Desmond Tutu, twentieth-century South African religious leader

Mark Twain, nineteenth-century American author

Irina Tweedie, twentieth-century English journalist

U

Miguel de Unamuno y Jugo, nineteenth-century Spanish philosopher and writer

Evelyn Underhill, nineteenth- and twentieth-century English mystic and writer

The *Upanishad*s, B.C.E. ninth- to fifth-century sacred Hindu texts

John Updike, twentieth-century American author

V

Henry Van Dyke, nineteenth-century American clergyman, educator, and author

Gerald Vann, author of *The Water and the Fire*, 1954

Vinaya, Mahavagga, ancient code of Buddhist monastic discipline

Vishnu, Puranas, ancient Hindu collection of legends

Swami Vivekananda, nineteenth-century Indian author

Voltaire, eighteenth-century French playwright and author

Marie Ebner von Eschenbach, nineteenth-century Austrian novelist

W

John J. Wade, author of *Conquering with Christ,* 1942

Barbara Ward, twentieth-century English economist, journalist, and conservationist

Robert Penn Warren, twentieth-century American author

Booker T. Washington, nineteenth-century American educator

Simone Weil, twentieth-century French philosopher and religious author

H. G. Wells, twentieth-century English author, sociologist, and historian

John Wesley, eighteenth-century English theologian, evangelist, and founder of Methodist church

Janwillem van de Wetering, twentieth-century Dutch author

Patrick White, twentieth-century American historian

Alfred North Whitehead, twentieth-century English mathematician and philosopher

Elie Wiesel, twentieth-century American Jewish philosopher and author

Oscar Wilde, nineteenth-century Irish poet, wit, and dramatist

Amos Wilder, twentieth-century American literary critic

Thornton Wilder, twentieth-century American novelist and playwright

John Alden Williams, twentieth-century American Islamic scholar

Charles Willie, twentieth-century African-American professor of education and urban studies

David Wolpe, twentieth-century American Jewish theologian and author

William Wordsworth, nineteenth-century English poet

Herman Wouk, twentieth-century American author

Y

Edward Young, eighteenth-century English poet

Z

R. C. Zaehner, twentieth-century English religion scholar

Hubert van Zeller, twentieth-century English Benedictine monk and author

Dogen Zenji, thirteenth-century Japanese Zen master

Heinrich Zimmer, nineteenth-century German Celtic scholar

Zitakala-Sa, nineteenth-century Native American writer

Index